A Report of the Royal College of Physicians and
the Royal College of Psychiatrists

The psychological care of medical patients

RECOGNITION OF NEED AND SERVICE PROVISION

ROYAL COLLEGE
OF PHYSICIANS

ROYAL COLLEGE
OF PSYCHIATRISTS

This report has been approved by the Councils of the Royal College of Physicians and the Royal College of Psychiatrists

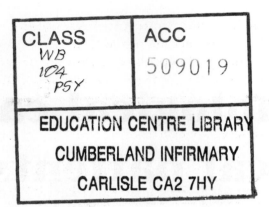
Royal College of Physicians of London
11 St Andrews Place, London NW1 4LE

Registered Charity No. 210508

Royal College of Psychiatrists
17 Belgrave Square, London SW1X 8PG

Registered Charity No. 228636

British Library Cataloguing-in-Publication Data
A catalogue record for this book is available from the British Library

Copyright © 1995 Royal College of Physicians and Royal College of Psychiatrists

ISBN 1 86016 016 6

Designed and typeset by the Royal College of Physicians Publications Unit
Printed in Great Britain by Cathedral Print Services Ltd, Salisbury

Foreword

As technological advances enable doctors to treat increasingly serious physical ill-nesses, it is essential that we do not neglect the psychological problems our patients encounter. The anxieties and feelings of depression that so often accompany many illnesses may become the principal determinant of a patient's quality of life. In addition, psychological disorders can cause bodily symptoms; these symptoms can lead to a costly but unrewarding search for organic disease while patients may not be receiving the psychological help they need.

Although general practitioners deal well with psychological disorders, recognition and treatment of these disorders after discharge from hospital is often poor.

The increasing emphasis on treatment for serious mental illness in the community must not prevent psychiatrists from contributing to the services which may improve the treatment of psychological disorders in the general hospital. There may be a cost reduction as well as health gains in providing specific liaison services; unrecognised and untreated psychiatric disorders may prolong hospital stay and lead to repeated unnecessary investigations for medically unexplained symptoms.

Many patients attend hospital following deliberate self-harm, or with alcohol related problems. There is therefore a good opportunity to contribute to the Health of the Nation targets of lower suicide rates and substance misuse by appropriate inter-vention and treatment of psychological disorders.

Our Colleges have recently collaborated in two conferences concerning the prob-lems of medical symptoms not explained by organic disease and of psychological disorders associated with physical disease. Previous reports have concerned the health risks associated with alcohol, and services for elderly mentally ill people.

This report from our two Colleges will stimulate training initiatives for all staff in the general hospital, including the psychiatrists who specialise in this area of work. We hope that specific liaison teams can be set up in each general hospital and that com-missioners in particular will support such proposals.

April 1995

FIONA CALDICOTT
President, Royal College of Psychiatrists

LESLIE TURNBERG
President, Royal College of Physicians

Joint working party on the Psychological Care of Medical Patients: Recognition of need and service provision

Sir Anthony M Dawson KCVO MD FRCP
Physician (Chairman)

Professor FH Creed FRCP FRCPsych
Professor of Psychiatry, University of Manchester (Honorary Secretary)

Ms Pam Hibbs
Formerly Chief Nursing Officer, St Bartholomew's Hospital

Mr JH James
Chief Executive, Kensington, Chelsea & Westminster Commissioning Agency

Mr J Keown
Senior Nurse, Psychiatric Services, Hackney Hospital

Dr Debra King MRCP(UK)
Senior Registrar in General & Geriatric Medicine, Clatterbridge Hospital, Wirral

Dr GP Maguire
Hon Consultant Psychiatrist, Christie Hospital NHS Trust, Manchester

Dr RA Mayou FRCP FRCPsych
Clinical Reader, University Department of Psychiatry, Warneford Hospital, Oxford

Professor ES Paykel MD FRCP FRCPsych
Professor of Psychiatry, Addenbrooke's Hospital, Cambridge

Dr GM Sterling MD FRCP
Consultant Physician, Southampton General Hospital

Professor JP Watson MD FRCP
Professor of Psychiatry, UMDS, Guy's Hospital, London

Ms Katharine Whitehorn
Journalist

Professor GK Wilcock MD FRCP
Professor in Care of the Elderly, University of Bristol

Dr D Kingdon
Department of Health Observer

Professor DR London DM FRCP
Registrar, Royal College of Physicians

Dr AP Hopkins MD FRCP
Director, Research Unit, Royal College of Physicians

Professor BL Pentecost MD FRCP
Formerly Linacre Fellow, Royal College of Physicians

In attendance:
Miss Elaine Stephenson BA, *Working Party Secretary*
Ms Barbara Coles MA, *Working Party Secretary*

Contents

SUMMARY AND RECOMMENDATIONS

Summary

1. This joint report has been produced in order to facilitate the development of services for patients with psychological disorders in the general hospital. The specific aims of the report are: (a) to impröve the ability of general hospital staff to detect these disorders and to increase their skills and confidence in managing them, and (b) to encourage purchasers to establish comprehensive liaison services in all provider units. These measures are expected to lead to an environment in which each patient's psychological and physical needs receive appropriate attention.

2. Psychological disorders occur frequently in the general hospital. Life-threatening or disabling physical illness may cause great distress; alternatively, especially in elderly people, the illness may directly affect brain function. In addition, some patients present with bodily symptoms that actually indicate underlying psychological disorder. Such patients are often very worried that an organic illness may be causing their symptoms and repeatedly request investigations; a few are seriously disturbed and at high risk of committing suicide. Other patients have alcohol or drug related problems or attend the hospital having deliberately harmed themselves. People with physical illness often have relationship or sexual problems which merit specific help.

3. Although common, psychological disorders may not be recognised and adequately dealt with in the general hospital. This is because (a) many interviews fail to elicit psychological problems, (b) modern medicine is orientated towards technological investigations which may divert attention away from psychological problems, and (c) many staff have not received adequate training or encouragement to pay sufficient attention to the psychological aspects of patient care. Such training and encouragement require the support of a liaison psychiatry team (psychiatrist, liaison nurses, social worker and psychologist) who must be readily available and appropriately skilled to provide rapid and comprehensive treatment when necessary.

4. A liaison psychiatry service, which improves treatment of psychological disorders in the general hospital, should:

   a reduce the number of investigations performed for physical symptoms that actually reflect underlying distress;

   b reduce length of hospital stay;

   c relieve symptoms of distress and improve the quality of life of some patients with serious physical illness; and

   d reduce the incidence of suicide and problem drinking in line with the *Health of the Nation* targets.

In order to achieve the above the working party makes the following recommendations:

Recommendations

Facilities

1   All inpatient and outpatient departments, including accident and emergency, must have private, quiet and safe facilities so that routine interviews can include a discussion of psychological problems.

History taking

2   All patients should be routinely asked direct questions about their mood, possible alcohol or drug misuse and, where appropriate, suicidal ideas. The results of these questions must be clearly recorded in the notes and brought to the attention of senior medical staff and the patient's GP.

Medical management and referral

3   Medical staff should know how to treat common psychological disorders, including how to develop a management plan for patients with medically unexplained symptoms, and understand how and when to refer a patient to the liaison psychiatry service.

Psychological assessment and treatment

4   Psychological assessment and appropriate treatment should be available for patients with unexplained physical symptoms, either within the hospital or from the primary care team. If such symptoms are numerous and persistent, a specific plan of management should be drawn up that includes limitation of hospital investigations and admissions.

Special services

5   A counselling service for alcohol problems should be readily available for both inpatients and outpatients.

6   The service for deliberate self-harm in each provider unit should be developed so that it conforms to the minimum standards set by the Royal College of Psychiatrists consensus statement.

Liaison psychiatry service

7   Purchasers should ensure that they purchase acute medical services in provider units, which include a liaison psychiatry service. The exact model for such a service will vary according to local circumstances but it must be consultant-led (at least five

sessions per week of specified consultant psychiatrist time), must include the range of skills required for such work and include a record-keeping system that allows regular audit of the service. Although managed within the mental health unit, the costs of this service should be included within the costs of each medical directorate service.

Training

8   The training of liaison psychiatrists, physicians and nurses should be improved so that their interviews with patients allow discussion of psychological problems and they have a full understanding of the importance of detection and management of psychological disorders throughout the general hospital. Such training should start at the undergraduate stage, be continued throughout general professional training and be offered as one aspect of continuing professional development.

Introduction

Background

1.1 The impetus for this report arose from a joint conference of the two Colleges on medical symptoms not explained by organic disease,[1] when it became apparent that services for patients with disorders of this type were not well developed at most hospitals. Two aspects came to light. First, most physicians manage patients with medically unexplained symptoms as best they can, but few have received specific training or are aware of recent research findings relevant to this important aspect of medical practice. Second, most physicians attending the conference agreed as to the need for a comprehensive liaison psychiatry service but many complained that, at their own hospital, this is confined to a service for deliberate self-harm patients with little additional service for other psychological problems.

Aims of this report

1.2 The aim of this report is to stimulate improvement in the psychological care of patients in the general hospital — both inpatients and outpatients. Such improvement will raise the overall quality of care for all patients and should also contribute to better outcome and reduced health care costs for the groups of patients whose disorders are outlined in Chapter 2. Improved psychological care may also contribute to the reduction of suicide set as one of the targets in *Health of the Nation*; such care will involve physicians, nurses, psychiatrists and psychologists, and continued care must also involve general practitioners.

The present situation

1.3 Psychological problems in the general hospital are common. There are some specialised services, for example for elderly people or for diabetics, that specifically address psychological disorders. More usually, psychological problems are not recognised and dealt with satisfactorily. Various factors contribute to the mishandling of such problems in the general hospital. These include:

- The medical outpatient clinic or ward may not provide the privacy and time for a discussion of psychological aspects of illness, so they tend to be ignored in the doctor-patient interaction.

- Modern medical practice is clearly orientated towards detecting and treating organic disease; this may divert attention away from psychological aspects. It is regarded as a greater error if a doctor fails to diagnose an organic disorder (in which treatment may not be very effective) than if a psychological disorder which may be considerably alleviated by appropriate treatment remains undiagnosed. This is in spite of Hippocratic teaching of the nervous element in the genesis of disease and the awareness of psychological disorders in the writings of physicians and the laity over the centuries.

- The diagnostic process relies heavily on technological investigations. These are expensive and may be misleading if they yield normal variations or abnormalities which are wrongly blamed for the patient's symptoms and disability. Repeated use of these investigations may reinforce the patient's fear that organic illness is being missed. Reliance on technological investigations usually means that psychological problems are discussed only at the end of the diagnostic search. If, eventually, the patient is told either that nothing is wrong or that no explanation can be found for the symptoms, the patient is likely to doubt the doctor's diagnostic ability and request referral to another doctor.

- The physician and nursing staff may not have received adequate training or developed sufficient skills to diagnose and manage complex psychological disorders, especially in those patients presenting with physical symptoms who initially deny anxiety or depression. Special techniques in history-taking may be required to reveal the underlying nature of the complaint. The physician, and other staff on a medical unit, may also be out of sympathy with such patients, partly through lack of understanding of their problems. Without appropriate training, staff may be reluctant to embark upon exploration of psychological problems in their patients unless expert psychiatric advice is readily available when required.[2]

1.4 One of the aims of this report is that physicians should be encouraged to develop more skills and confidence in managing psychological aspects of illness as part of routine care; this can be achieved only if referral to a psychologist or psychiatrist can be expedited when necessary. A liaison psychiatry team should be involved in the training of nurses and doctors and should help to develop an environment in which the psychological needs of patients are adequately addressed.

Liaison psychiatry services

1.5 Most district general hospitals do not have a full liaison psychiatry service, ie one that caters for a broad range of psychological problems as well as providing a service for deliberate self-harm patients. Less than half the districts surveyed by Mayou *et al*[3] had a designated consultant psychiatrist with overall responsibility for the general hospital service; very few had a full liaison psychiatry team. This is in sharp contrast to some other European countries that have a liaison psychiatry service in each district hospital.[4] It is hoped that this report will encourage purchasers to buy comprehensive liaison psychiatry services throughout the UK.

1.6 There is competition for scarce resources between hospital and community psychiatric services, and over recent years there has been greater emphasis on community developments than on liaison psychiatry services.[5] There are conflicts of time and priorities. Where there are insufficient psychiatrists,[6] management of major psychotic illness in the community may take precedence over general hospital work, even though there is some evidence that patients referred to psychiatrists within the general hospital may have similar disorders to those referred by GPs.[7]

1.7   The training of psychiatrists usually includes general hospital psychiatry but this may not include training in the difficult diagnostic and management problems that make this work so demanding of the psychiatrist. To increase training opportunities in liaison psychiatry is a further aim of this report.[8]

Models of service

Liaison psychiatry

1.8   The work of a psychiatrist in a general hospital has been named *liaison psychiatry* following the type of clinical practice developed in the USA, where the psychiatrist attends medical ward rounds and other clinical meetings. This model has proved expensive on the psychiatrist's time and is now being used less frequently in the USA, even though it may be beneficial on renal, intensive care and similar units.

Consultation

1.9   The alternative model is that of *consultation*, where each patient on whom an opinion is sought is referred to the psychiatrist. The problem with this model is that the psychiatrist may visit the ward and see the patient without the physician being present, so his/her report may not answer the particular points that led to the referral.

Consultation-liaison

1.10   A compromise arrangement has therefore been reached, in which individual consultation takes place, but where the psychiatrist and physician meet regularly to discuss individual patients and general aspects of patient care; the term *consultation-liaison* has been applied and is now popular with many American and European psychiatrists who specialise in this type of work. For the purposes of this report 'liaison' will be used alone for brevity and, because it is well recognised, the term 'liaison psychiatry' will be used. However, the report concerns the wide range of psychological problems seen in the general hospital and is not confined solely to psychiatric disorders.

Scope of this report

1.11   It must be recognised that all illnesses carry both physical and psychological features. This report is concerned with two aspects. First, the general measures we recommend are intended to change the milieu in which doctors and nurses interact with their patients so that greater recognition will be given to the usual psychological reactions to illness and hospitalisation. Second, the more pronounced psychological problems and formal psychiatric disorders will be discussed; these may exacerbate or cause bodily symptoms and complicate patient care. It is intended that the development of a liaison psychiatry team, in addition to providing a consultation service, will lead to changes in outpatient and inpatient medical care, including aspects of ward organisation and staff relationships. Attitudes or conflicts and communication difficulties may be highlighted; they may involve patient, relatives, staff, management and the general practitioner. This wider context may be seen as a by-product of the development of the liaison psychiatry team. It should produce measurable changes in patient management.

1.12   Many who read the report will not have detailed knowledge of some of the relevant clinical techniques. For this reason the report carries a number of appendices which include background literature and descriptions of clinical methods.

1.13   The report deliberately retains as its focus the psychological problems which are frequently encountered within general medical services of the general hospital which include, for example, occupational health and other medical subspecialties. The working party did not address the more specific problems encountered in specialties such as surgery and obstetrics and gynaecology, though many aspects of this document can readily be applied to them. The report has been written with specific reference to medical patients but the development of a liaison psychiatry team is likely to lead to improvement of services generally and not solely for medical patients. The report is not concerned with primary care and services for children and adolescents. It refers only briefly to services for elderly people as these have been considered in other reports. A model of liaison for geriatricians and old age psychiatrists is given in Appendix F; in many respects liaison in these areas is better developed than in general medicine.

1.14   One aspect of improved liaison between psychiatrists and physicians is that patients under the care of a psychiatrist should have their medical problems recognised and treated more satisfactorily.

1.15   The emphasis of this report is on the individual patient. It is recognised that good psychological care also involves assessment and help, where necessary, for patients' relatives or other informal carers. This is especially important with chronically ill patients; assessment of a patient's state in this report should also be taken to indicate assessment of any problems affecting the carer.

Chapter 1
Summary and recommendations

1 The purpose of this report is to stimulate improvements in the services for psychological disorders in the general hospital. Although they are common, psychological disorders may not be recognised and treated in the general hospital because many interviews with patients fail to elicit psychological problems. This comes about because modern medicine is orientated towards technological investigations which may divert attention away from psychological problems and because many staff have not received adequate training or encouragement to pay sufficient attention to the psychological aspects of patient care (para 1.3).

2 Comprehensive psychological care of patients in the general hospital requires a liaison psychiatry team (psychiatrist, liaison nurses, social worker and psychologist) who must be readily available and appropriately skilled to provide rapid and comprehensive treatment when necessary (para 1.5). Further training of liaison psychiatrists for this purpose is necessary (para 1.7).

3 The specific recommendations of this report include measures to improve the ability of general hospital staff to detect these disorders, to increase their skills and confidence in managing them and to encourage purchasers to develop comprehensive liaison services in all provider units (para 1.4). These measures are expected to lead to an environment in which each patient's psychological and physical needs receive appropriate attention.

Further Reading

LLOYD G. *Textbook of general hospital psychiatry.* Edinburgh: Churchill Livingstone, 1991.

CASSEM NH, ed. *Massachusetts General Hospital handbook of general hospital psychiatry*, 3rd edn. St. Louis: Mosby Year Book, 1991.

GOLDBERG DP, BENJAMIN S, CREED F. *Psychiatry in medical practice.* 2nd edn. London, New York: Routledge, 1991.

BENJAMIN S, HOUSE A, JENKINS P, eds. *Liaison psychiatry: defining needs and planning services.* London: Gaskell, 1994.

CREED FH, GUTHRIE E, eds. *College seminars: liaison psychiatry.* London: Gaskell, in press.

CREED F, PFEFFER JM. *Medicine and psychiatry: a practical approach.* London: Pitman, 1984.

Chapter 2

Interface between the physical and psychological aspects of medicine

Introduction

2.1 There are social and psychological aspects of all illnesses, as well as physical ones; optimal care will be achieved if the patient is treated in an environment where staff are sensitive to, and able to deal with, all of these aspects. This chapter identifies some specific areas where psychiatric and physical disorders overlap, indicates their frequency and highlights relevant aspects of management. Later chapters will indicate general measures which will aid the detection and management of specific psychological problems as well as stimulate better care for patients with a broad range of psychosocial problems in the general hospital.

2.2 Table 2.1 indicates ways in which physical and psychological disorders overlap. Sections A and B refer to those conditions where the primary disorder is physical (eg arthritis, cancer, Parkinson's disease) but where important secondary psychological symptoms occur either as the result of direct alteration of brain function (eg delirium; category B in Table 2.1) or when the physical illness leads to serious problems of adjustment or depression (category A). In other categories the primary disorder is psychological, which may present to the doctor with bodily symptoms such as pain or breathing difficulties (C1), as liver damage caused by heavy drinking (D), or as a result of ingestion of paracetamol (E). Areas which have been covered by previous reports (alcohol misuse, services for elderly people) are not covered in detail in this chapter.

Organic disease and associated psychiatric disorder

2.3 Patients often become miserable and upset in response to physical illness and hospitalisation, and it may be difficult to decide when a psychiatric disorder has developed. The common reactions to physical illness are adjustment, anxiety and depressive disorders. There are now standardised criteria for diagnosing psychiatric disorders, the best recognised being the International Classification of Diseases (ICD-10)[9] and the Diagnostic and Statistical Manual (DSM-IV).[10] The definitions of the psychiatric disorders seen in the general hospital are summarised in Appendices A and B. Clinical practice is concerned, however, with all aspects of psychological, behavioural and social problems even when these do not constitute a specific psychiatric disorder.

Table 2.1

Classification of psychiatric and psychological problems that may be encountered in general medical units

Category	Sub Category
A Organic disease with associated psychiatric disorder	1 Adjustment disorder 2 Anxiety disorder 3 Depressive disorder
B Cerebral complications of organic disease	1 Delirium 2 Dementia 3 Focal defects: personality or perceptual changes

C Bodily symptoms not due to organic disease (medically unexplained symptoms)	1 Stress reactions/fears of illness and somatic presentation of anxiety and depressive disorders (somatisation)
	2 Chronic multiple unexplained symptoms (chronic somatisation),
	    a Somatoform disorders
	    b Simulated disorders

D Patients who abuse alcohol and drugs	1 As a cause of admission 2 Detected during inpatient stay
E Deliberate self-harm (DSH)	1 Inpatients following DSH 2 Outpatients seen in A & E
F Patients with sexual or relationship problems or eating disorders	1 Direct presentation 2 Complicating other disease (eg diabetes)

Adjustment, anxiety and depressive disorders

2.4   Adjustment disorders occur in approximately one-quarter of general medical patients. Anxiety and depressive disorders occur in a further 12–16% (Table 2.2) which is at least twice as high as the prevalence of these disorders in the general population. The prevalence of anxiety and depressive disorders is particularly high (25–35%) in the following groups:[11,12]

■   Illnesses affecting the brain, eg stroke

■   Acute painful and/or life-threatening illness, eg myocardial infarction, malignancy

■   Chronic, painful, disabling or disfiguring illness which impedes self-care, eg rheumatoid arthritis

Table 2.2
Prevalence of psychiatric disorders in 453 medical inpatients[12]

Psychiatric disorder	All patients		Affected patients only	
	Men (%)	Women (%)	Recognised by house physician (%)	Referred to psychiatrist (%)
Anxiety/depression	12 *(4–6)	16 *(8–10)	44	7.6
Alcohol problems	18	4	40	4.5
Dementia and delirium (patients over 70 years only)	23	38	Not recorded	15

* Expected figures in general population

■ Major and unpleasant treatments, eg chemotherapy

■ Elderly people.

2.5 Anxiety and/or depressive disorders in association with physical illness may:

■ Impair the patient's quality of life through increased pain, worsened disability and lowered mood, which may occasionally be accompanied by suicidal ideas.

■ Delay recovery (examples are depressive disorder after a stroke and anxiety following a heart attack, which, if untreated, hinder rehabilitation). Depression following myocardial infarction may be associated with worse angina and increased mortality.[13,14]

■ Increase the chance of problematic illness behaviour; examples are patients with rheumatoid arthritis or inflammatory bowel disease who attend the clinic frequently, consume large quantities of analgesics, worry about their illness and become resistant to the doctor's reassurance.[15-17]

Better recognition and management of psychiatric disorders in the physically ill therefore carry the potential to improve a patient's quality of life, to reduce disability and distress, to reduce length of stay in hospital and frequency of outpatient attendances and reduce suicidal risk.

Cerebral complications of organic disease: dementia and delirium

2.6 Dementia and delirium are predominantly, but not solely, found in elderly people, for whom the overlap between physical and psychiatric disorders is particularly prominent; 20–40% of patients admitted to either geriatric or old age psychiatric units suffer from a mixture of medical and psychiatric conditions.[18] Delirium is detected in at least 10% of those admitted to hospital with acute illness,[19] and is most likely in those who also have dementia, defective hearing and vision, Parkinson's disease and are of advanced age; precipitating factors include pneumonia, cardiac failure, urinary infection, carcinomatosis, hypocalcaemia and drugs. It is not surprising, therefore, that significantly increased death rates have been reported for patients who have been delirious at some point during their hospital stay.

2.7   Between one-quarter and one-third of elderly medical inpatients have dementia.[18] The significance of this is that, as well as requiring appropriate care, such patients stay considerably longer in hospital than those who are not cognitively impaired. This may be attributable in part to lack of suitable accommodation following discharge but it also reflects the fact that cognitive impairment limits compliance with medication, making management more complex; improved services for patients with cognitive impairment lead to decreased length of stay (para 5.5). Services for these patients have been described in a previous joint report,[20] *Care of elderly people with mental illness: specialist services and medical training,* to which the reader is referred.

Bodily symptoms not due to organic disease (medically unexplained symptoms)

Unexplained bodily symptoms in patients attending medical clinics

2.8   Between a quarter and half of new medical outpatients experience bodily symptoms that cannot be explained on the basis of organic disease; they are given a diagnosis of a recognisable syndrome (such as irritable bowel syndrome or chronic fatigue syndrome) or of 'ill-defined symptoms and signs'.[1,21-23] The most common symptoms are fatigue, chest pain, dizziness, headache, back pain, abdominal pain.[24] Reasons for attendance at the medical clinics may not be related to either organic or psychiatric disorder; they include social isolation, recent social stress, attitudes to illness in general and, particularly, worry that the symptoms represent serious organic disease.[25] The last often leads to numerous investigations aimed at 'reassuring the patient' but may not be successful in this respect.[26]

2.9   Up to half the patients presenting with unexplained bodily symptoms have underlying anxiety or depressive disorders (see Table 2.3, upper row), which may pass unrecognised in the medical clinic.[22,27-29] The term 'somatisation' has been used to describe this physical presentation of psychological disorder.[30-32] Some of the patients who present in this way readily admit to feelings of anxiety and depression *if asked directly* — so-called 'facultative somatisers'.[33] Other patients do not admit to depressed mood but have physical symptoms of depressive disorder — so-called 'masked depression'[34,35] (see Appendix A); there may be current life stresses or a family history of depressive disorder, and the symptoms may respond to antidepressants.

Table 2.3
Prevalence of psychiatric disorders in medical outpatients according to final medical diagnosis[37]

Psychiatric diagnosis	Definite organic diagnosis (%) n = 91	Recognised syndromes (eg irritable bowel syndrome, fibromyalgia) (%) n = 42	No organic diagnosis (%) n = 58
Anxiety/depression	12	43	33
Somatisation/hypochondriasis	5	21	16

2.10   The diagnosis and investigation of these medically unexplained symptoms demands a high degree of diagnostic acumen and facilities that enable the staff to investigate psychosocial problems as readily as organic diseases. Sometimes patients must be kept under periodic observation until the cause of the symptoms is clear; in one series of new outpatients a quarter came within this category.[36] Simple but effective strategies are needed to deal with these specific problems.[37]

Chronic multiple unexplained symptoms (chronic somatisation, somatoform and conversion disorders)

2.11   A smaller proportion of patients presenting to the medical clinics have chronic physical symptoms, in numerous bodily systems, which are distressing and disabling but which cannot be explained on the basis of organic disease (see Table 2.3, lower row). Such patients may cause considerable unease in doctors who may repeatedly perform fruitless investigations. This small group of patients therefore uses a disproportionate amount of health service resources.[38,39]

2.12   The recent diagnostic schemes ICD-10 and DSM-IV have grouped together the overlapping 'somatoform disorders', which are listed in Table 2.4. These disorders have much in common with each other and differ only in the emphasis of their presentation. The simulated disorders have some features in common and are also included in this section.

2.13   The chronic somatising disorders have in common 'chronic abnormal illness behaviour'. This term describes those behaviours that reflect an individual's excessive concern about underlying physical disease and the consequent search for medical treatment which may be quite out of proportion to the realistic chance of finding an organic cause for the symptoms. This group of patients may become seriously disabled and put extreme pressure on doctors to perform investigations. Doctors should resist the temptation to continue investigating for organic disease unless they feel that such an eventual diagnosis is a serious possibility.

Table 2.4

Classification of somatoform and simulated disorders

	Clinical features
Chronic somatising disorders	
Somatisation disorder	※ 2 years of multiple/variable physical symptoms for which no adequate physical explanation can be found
	※ Persistent refusal to accept reassurance from doctor
	※ Impairment in social function as a result of the symptoms
Somatoform pain disorder	※ Persistent pain unexplained by organic disorder or physiological process
Hypochondriacal disorder	※ Persistent preoccupation with possibility of serious disease
	※ Refusal to accept reassurance from doctor and results of normal investigation
Simulated disorders	
Dissociative (conversion) disorders	※ Acute onset of dramatic symptom(s) which mimic organic disease
	※ Unconscious simulation
Malingering	※ Feigned illness
	※ Conscious motivation to avoid responsibility
Factitious disorders	※ Self-induced symptoms and signs
	※ Patient aware of the deception but has little insight into underlying motivation (unlike malingerer)
	※ Includes Münchausen syndrome (and 'by proxy')

Frequency and costs of medically unexplained symptoms

The community

2.14   The largest epidemiological study suggests that 0.3% of a USA population have *chronic multiple unexplained symptoms*.[40] Because of their very high utilisation of medical resources, the total health care costs for this small group of the population were calculated to be $4,700 per annum, nine times the US average. The figure of 0.3% represents 1,200 people in a health district of 400,000 population. Using a less conservative definition of unexplained medical symptoms, 4.4% of the population (17,600 in a district of 400,000) would be regarded as having somatisation. Approximately 50% of these patients have a concurrent diagnosis of depression or anxiety.[41] There is therefore a large reservoir of patients who may present physical symptoms to the GP and be referred to the general hospital for investigations.

The clinic

2.15 In a study of the patients attending a medical outpatient clinic in the USA, 567 new symptoms were recorded; 382 of these were fully evaluated and 37 turned out to be due to definite organic disease.[24] The average cost per evaluation was $218 per symptom. The cost per organic diagnosis ranged from over $7,000 for headaches and back pain to $1,000 for impotence and cough (average $2,252). UK studies indicate the high proportion of new patients who have somatising disorders.[42] Fears have been expressed that the current changes in the NHS, with fund-holding GPs and open access investigations, will lead to more referrals for investigations and increased cost but no better service to patients.[43,44]

Hospital admissions

2.16 In a detailed Danish study, Fink[45,46] identified 1% of the general population who had been admitted 10 times or more to general hospitals during an eight-year period. They had accumulated over 3,000 such admissions of which 1,321 were for verifiable organic diagnoses, 1,126 were medically unexplained and 576 were the result of self-destructive acts, alcoholism, drug dependence and complications of these (eg chronic hepatitis, chronic pancreatitis). A small group of persistent somatisers (representing 760 persons in a district of 400,000 population) had, during their lifetime, a median of 22 general hospital admissions for which no medical explanation could be found.

Referrals to the liaison psychiatrist

2.17 Somatisation accounts for approximately one-third of referrals to liaison psychiatrists.[7,47,48] In one study, the costs of investigation prior to referral ranged from £2,300 to £25 (median £286).[49] Most patients referred in this way respond to a combination of psychological treatments and antidepressants but some patients may require many hours of treatment.[7,47] Even on current referral patterns there are at least 100 such patients referred per annum to the liaison service of a large hospital; with increasing recognition of somatic presentations of psychological disorders this number is likely to increase.

Patients who misuse alcohol and drugs

2.18 Substance misuse problems are common in both outpatients and inpatients. Approximately 20% of male inpatients have alcohol-related problems (Table 2.2); the proportion is higher in inner city areas.[50-55] For half the patients who misuse alcohol the illness leading to admission is directly alcohol-related.[56] Alcohol misuse is of such importance that it has given rise to four Royal College reports, to which the reader is referred.[57-60] Alcohol problems are unlikely to be detected unless specifically screened for. Intervention should be effective in achieving the *Health of the Nation* target for the reduction of problem drinking.

2.19 The interaction of physical illness and psychosocial difficulties in patients who abuse alcohol may be complex. Alcohol withdrawal is a common cause of delirium; it may precipitate a general hospital admission or occur following admission for another reason. Self-injury is common in this population. Alcohol may cause physical illness, eg liver disease, and complicate care because it is associated with poor compliance with medical treatment. In addition, problems occur because some alcohol misusers live disorganised lives, have poor general health and are alienated from the primary and specialist medical services. There is a very important opportunity to start treatment for alcohol dependence while such patients are in the medical ward, but considerable behavioural and management problems may occur if these patients, while suffering from life-threatening alcohol related physical illness, refuse to accept that they need help.

Similar problems occur with drug misuse; Ghodse[61] estimated that 18.3 per 1,000 attendances at accident and emergency departments in London were drug related. The same overlap between physical and psychological problems exists as with alcohol.[62]

Deliberate self-harm patients

2.20 Deliberate self-harm remains the most common reason for admission of young people to hospital, with approximately 100,000 episodes per year in England and Wales. In addition, many patients are seen in the accident and emergency department and are discharged without being admitted. Although physicians may have received specific training which enables them to take responsibility for the psychiatric aspects of care, that training may not be satisfactory; for example, case notes do not always include vital information about suicidal risk.[63,64]

2.21 Improved services for self-harm patients should lead to:

a better detection and management of those at risk of suicide and hence help to meet the *Health of the Nation* target of reducing suicide rates (see para 7.2);

b better social adjustment and personal well-being following the deliberate self-harm, with reduced chances of repetition of deliberate self-harm.[65]

Sexual or relationship problems and eating disorders

2.22 Slag *et al*[66] surveyed 1,000 male medical outpatients, 34% of whom were impotent. In 14% there was a psychogenic cause; in the remainder, medication was the commonest cause, followed by hypogonadism, diabetes mellitus, neurological, urological and vascular disorders. In a group presenting with impotence, Melman *et al*[67] found that in 40% it had a psychogenic cause, in 30% it was a purely organic disorder and the remainder had a combination of the two. Full accounts of the subject are given by Kirby *et al*[68] and Hawton.[69]

2.23   Sexual problems among women may present with a variety of bodily symptoms, including irritable bowel syndrome[70] and chronic pain.[71] There is increasing concern that such presentations represent former sexual abuse[72] which can only be elicited by sensitive and detailed interviewing. The subject is reviewed in Bancroft[73] and Briere.[74] Greater awareness of the sexual problems encountered by patients with physical illness will lead to better quality of care; adjustment of medication or referral for psychosexual counselling will help the majority.

2.24   Like alcohol problems, eating disorders (anorexia nervosa, bulimia nervosa and overeating), though often undisclosed by the patient, may be the sole explanation for medically unexplained symptoms such as weight change, vomiting, abdominal or menstrual complaints. Associated laxative abuse may lead to diarrhoea, weakness or hypokalaemia. Alternatively eating disorders may complicate conditions such as diabetes, when very difficult management problems may occur. Patients are characteristically reluctant to admit to having an eating disorder; doctors need to have a high index of suspicion, interview patients with skill, understanding and concern and be prepared to investigate and manage the problem through systematic observation, interviews with relatives and involvement of the liaison psychiatric team. Patients with eating disorders are at high risk of concurrent depression, substance misuse and suicide.

Psychiatric disorders and utilisation of medical services

2.25   Several studies have demonstrated the close overlap of physical and psychiatric disorders in terms of service use. Mayou et al[75] found that patients admitted to medical wards had a higher rate of contact with psychiatric services (compared with the expected rate) during the two years before and after the medical admission. This was not confined to selected diagnostic groups — it reflects the positive association of physical and psychiatric disorders, which has also been demonstrated in community studies. Fink noted that patients with a past history of psychiatric treatment had significantly longer general hospital admissions.[46] Katon et al found that half the patients who were high utilisers of general medical health services had psychiatric disorders — 23% had depressive disorders, 22% anxiety disorders and 20% somatisation.[76] The Pathways to Care study[77] indicated that approximately a quarter of all new patients reaching a district psychiatric service did so via the general hospital, either through the accident and emergency department or through other inpatient or outpatient departments.

Chapter 2
Summary and recommendations

1   Psychological disorders occur frequently in the general hospital. Life-threatening or disabling physical illness may cause great distress; alternatively, especially in elderly people, the illness may directly affect brain function. In addition, some patients present with bodily symptoms which actually indicate underlying psychological disorder; such patients are often very worried about the possibility of physical illness causing their symptoms and request investigations. Other patients have alcohol or drug related problems or attend the hospital having deliberately harmed themselves. People with physical illness often have relationship or sexual problems which merit specific help (Tables 2.2, 2.3).

2   The psychiatric disorders are often persistent and increase the suicide risk. They are in themselves unpleasant and reduce quality of life (para 2.5).

3   Medically unexplained symptoms, especially when chronic, are expensive because of excessive investigations and increased length of stay in hospital (paras 2.14–2.16).

4   Problems related to drugs, alcohol and deliberate self-harm are common areas where patients may require concurrent psychiatric and physical assessment or treatment (paras 2.18, 2.20, 2.21). Improved care of these patients will contribute to specific *Health of the Nation* targets.

5   Since psychological disorders deserve detection and appropriate management within the general hospital, it is recommended that:

   a   Treatment should be provided primarily by the physician and other staff in the general hospital with the back-up of the liaison psychiatry team for selected cases.

   b   A psychiatric service should be responsive, offering rapid assessment when appropriate, always by a member of the psychiatric team who is adequately trained and experienced to make such an assessment.

   c   Assessment of quality of care in the general hospital should always include measurement of psychological as well as physical aspects (paras 2.5, 2.22, 2.23).

Further Reading

BASS C, ed. *Somatisation: physical symptoms and psychological disorder.* Oxford: Blackwell Scientific Publications, 1990.

HAWTON K, CATALAN J. *Attempted suicide: practical guide to its nature and management,* 2nd edn. Oxford: Oxford University Press, 1987.

JENKINS P, JAMIL N. The need for specialist services for mood disorders in the medically ill. In: Benjamin S, House A, Jenkins P, eds. *Liaison psychiatry: defining needs and planning services.* London: Gaskell, 1994:24–33.

SHARPE M, MAYOU R, BASS C. *Functional somatic symptoms.* Oxford: Oxford University Press, 1995. In press.

Chapter 3
Recognising psychological problems

Failure to recognise psychological disorders in the general hospital

3.1 Psychiatric disorders, though common in the general hospital, frequently go undetected by medical staff (Table 2.2).[11,12, 78] Increased recognition of psychological problems would improve the quality of care as has been shown in the previous chapter. In the case of alcohol problems and deliberate self-harm, guidelines already exist concerning assessment by those specifically trained for this purpose (see paras 3.14, 3.15); adherence to these guidelines is far from satisfactory. In the case of anxiety, depression and sexual problems, the mode of interviewing is important.[33] Some patients, for example those with allergy, may resort to complementary medicine when in fact psychological treatment is required for an underlying psychological problem. Patients with factitious disorders and some patients with eating disorders go to extraordinary lengths to hide their activities, so recognising the problem requires a great deal of skill and usually involves several members of staff.

3.2 Studies of recognition have shown that physicians and nurses tend to overestimate the incidence and extent of anxiety disorders but seriously underestimate the incidence and severity of depressive disorders.[79-81] The latter are often dismissed as an understandable reaction to physical illness. Nursing staff tend to recognise depressive disorders more frequently than medical staff but still recognised only 50% in one study.[80]

3.3 It has been demonstrated repeatedly that doctors fail to identify the high alcohol consumption of many of their patients.[57,82,83] Junior doctors commonly regard this information as low priority.[83] This means that the opportunity to help these problem drinkers is lost; since counselling on the medical ward leads to a significant reduction of alcohol consumption, current practice should be changed.[84,85]

Reasons why psychological disorders are not recognised

3.4 Patients with alcohol problems and somatisation may deliberately conceal their psychological difficulties, but patients with a broad range of physical illnesses are also unlikely to disclose their psychological problems unless asked direct questions that signal the doctor's or nurse's interest in these areas.[86-89] Patients with serious physical illness tend to consider mood disturbance, body image problems or sexual problems inevitable consequences of the illness or its treatment and do not wish to trouble the busy staff for fear of being considered troublesome or inadequate.[89] For their part, doctors and nurses tend to use strategies that keep them at a safe distance from the patients' problems, even when faced with clear indicators of upset, worry or sexual problems.

3.5　These distancing strategies appear to be used by all health professionals looking after the physically ill, regardless of their discipline or experience. When faced with the patient's concerns, doctors and nurses tend to:

- 'jolly' the patient along by explaining away the distress as normal;

- offer advice before the problem has been fully understood;

- offer false reassurance; and

- switch the discussion to safer topics. Staff do this because they are afraid that direct questions might release strong emotions in the patient, which they would find difficult to handle, and might lead the patient to ask questions about treatment options and duration of remaining life, which they would find difficult to answer.[90]

3.6　Many staff report that they have been inadequately trained and have too little time to interview their patients in depth. Some express particular concerns that direct interviewing will bring them too close to their patients' suffering, which might then affect their own feelings and make it more difficult for them to cope with the stress of caring for seriously ill patients. Other factors include difficult work schedules, poor control of physical symptoms, conflict with colleagues and negative attitudes of senior staff which encourage nurses to use distancing strategies; on the other hand, knowing that the senior sister has an interest in psychological aspects of care provides a positive influence.[91,92]

Improving recognition of psychological disorders in the physically ill

Methods of interviewing

3.7　A number of features should be present for all medical consultations that will help the physician in a busy clinic to detect psychiatric disorders:

- Privacy is essential; a private interview room where sensitive topics can be tackled without fear of interruption must be available to all staff for this purpose

- Adequate time is essential, though the frequently held misapprehension that this type of interview must necessarily be lengthy should be dispelled[89]

- The patient must be interviewed, if possible, both with and without a relative present

- The doctor should ask direct questions about psychological difficulties and, at the first interview, explore clues suggesting psychological distress.

Use of non-medical staff

3.8　One approach to improving recognition of psychological disorders has been to appoint key nurses and social workers, train them in the appropriate interviewing and assessment skills and offer them ongoing support and supervision. For cancer patients this approach did not prevent anxiety, depression, body image problems and sexual difficulties but did greatly increase the detection rate and referral for specialist help: 76% of patients with psychological problems were referred compared with 15% previously. The special help led to a three- to four-fold reduction in the prevalence of psychiatric disorder.[93]

3.9   A danger of the specialist nurse approach is that clinicians and other nurses will leave all the psychological care to the specialist nurses. Hence, attention should be given to ways of upgrading the skills of all doctors and nurses. Improved interview skills increase recognition of the psychological problems associated with physical illness and medically unexplained symptoms.[94]

Training

3.10   Workshops have been developed to help experienced doctors and nurses improve their interviewing and assessment skills as well as their ability to deal with particularly difficult situations, for example breaking bad news and being asked difficult questions.[94] Such training means that staff are more likely to ask directly about patients' psychological concerns as well as physical complaints, and are less likely to offer reassurance and advice prematurely.[95] Training may also be focused on detection of psychological problems in patients presenting with physical symptoms.[33,96] The training courses have confirmed that even very experienced doctors and nurses can greatly improve their confidence in interviewing and their ability to recognise and manage psychiatric disorders.

Screening questionnaires

3.11   *Anxiety and depression:* The likelihood of psychological disorder can be assessed using self-administered questionnaires (see Appendix C). However, while these are useful for population surveys, when an estimate of the prevalence of psychiatric disorder is required, their use is more limited with individual patients, many of whom cannot answer self-administered questionnaires unaided.[97] In addition, the threshold of self-administered questionnaires indicating probable psychiatric disorder is considerably higher in the physically ill than for the general population. In the individual patient, self-administered questionnaires are usually little more than pointers for further questioning. Most psychiatric disorders can only be diagnosed in the individual patient by clinical interview.[98]

3.12   *Dementia:* Screening questionnaires such as the Mini-Mental State and the Newcastle Scale (see Appendix C) are widely used for detecting cognitive impairment. Low scores on these scales can be due to dementia but also to delirium, psychosis and depression. Interpretation of questionnaire results therefore requires further evaluation. Nursing staff might in some circumstances use such tests routinely, informing medical staff when low scores are noted.

Alcohol and drug related problems

3.13   Recognition of alcohol or drug misuse is greatly aided by a high index of suspicion. Detailed history-taking is essential for all patients with alcohol related conditions and for any patient who has strange or atypical symptoms; these often turn out to have alcohol, drug or factitious disorders as their underlying cause. The key clinical skills are routinely screening for alcohol problems, taking a detailed drinking history when necessary and examining patients for signs of alcohol induced liver disease or of drug taking, such as injection sites.

3.14   For screening for alcohol misuse, the widely used CAGE questionnaire is recommended:

> Have you ever felt that you should CUT down on your drinking?
>
> Have other people ANNOYED you by criticising your drinking?
>
> Have you ever felt GUILTY about your drinking?
>
> Have you ever had a drink first thing in the morning to steady your nerves or get rid of a hangover (an EYEOPENER)?

A positive answer to any **two** of these questions should lead to a detailed drinking history (a score of 2 or more means a 45% probability of problem drinking). See also Appendix C.

3.15   The Royal College of Physicians[57] recommended that every person seen in general practice or in hospital should be asked about his or her alcohol intake as a matter of routine, along with questions about medication, and the answers recorded. This aim has not yet been achieved and should therefore be closely audited until it is achieved.

Assessment of patients following deliberate self-harm

3.16   The Department of Health recommendations[99] make it clear that all self-harm patients being discharged from hospital, whether from inpatient wards or accident and emergency departments, require a psychosocial assessment 'by staff specifically trained for this task'. Four groups of staff commonly perform these assessments: general medical staff, psychiatrists, psychiatric nurses and social workers. All require specific training.[100]

3.17   It is recommended that each hospital should have a designated group of professional staff responsible for the planning and implementation of services for this category of patients.[99] This group has the responsibility for ensuring adequate assessments and recognition of psychiatric disorders and serious social problems. These assessments are not always adequate, however.[63] In view of the *Health of the Nation* target to reduce the suicide rate, these services must be very carefully planned and audited as they deal with the population at greatest risk of eventually committing suicide. Details of how these services can be audited have recently been produced by the Royal College of Psychiatrists.[100] An important aspect of the assessment is whether the patient should be referred to the psychiatric service.

Sexual and body image problems

3.18   Sexual and body image problems are often avoided by doctors and patients during clinical interviews for reasons of social embarrassment. In fact, most patients are enormously relieved when asked directly about sexual difficulties as they may not have been previously discussed, even with the spouse. Body image problems may also become apparent if the patient is asked how they feel about the illness and the way it affects their body. Such questions should be asked routinely of patients who undergo mutilating surgery, have a stoma, experience marked weight loss, muscle wasting or paralysis.

Special groups of patients

3.19   Recognition of psychological disorders may be especially difficult in elderly people, people with learning difficulties and people from ethnic minority groups. The problem is not simply one of language; somatic presentation of psychological disorders is especially likely in these groups and a careful history from an informant will often be necessary in addition to the history from, and examination of, the patient.

Chapter 3
Summary and recommendations

Detection of psychological disorders in the general hospital may be inadequate. The current guidelines regarding alcohol and drug related problems and the assessment of deliberate self-harm patients are not always adhered to (paras 3.15, 3.16). Recognition of other psychological problems requires a different style of interviewing, improved facilities and better training of staff. It is therefore recommended that :

a All inpatient and outpatient facilities must allow routine interviews to be conducted in privacy for exploring psychological problems (paras 1.3, 3.7).

b Nurses, physicians and psychiatrists should be able to detect anxiety and depressive disorders, sexual and body image problems and substance misuse even if these are initially denied by the patient (para 3.10). They should be aware of the scales used to assess cognitive function, depression and, where appropriate, degree of suicidal intent (paras 3.11, 3.12).

c Nursing or other staff should bring to the attention of physicians any patients whom they find to be markedly depressed, have suicidal ideas, a poor memory or a substance misuse problem (paras 3.11, 3.12, 3.15, 3.17). All such problems should be routinely entered into the case notes in a way that facilitates audit of subsequent care.

d Each provider unit should ensure that it has appropriately trained staff to assess deliberate self-harm patients and that the notes of these patients are regularly reviewed and thoroughly assessed (paras 3.16, 3.17).

Further Reading

MAGUIRE P, FAULKNER A. How to improve the counselling skills of doctors and nurses in cancer care. *British Medical Journal* 1988; **297**: 847–9

ROYAL COLLEGE OF PHYSICIANS. *A great and growing evil: the medical consequences of alcohol abuse.* London: Tavistock, 1987.

ROYAL COLLEGE OF PSYCHIATRISTS. *Alcohol: our favourite drug.* London: Tavistock, 1986.

ROYAL COLLEGE OF PSYCHIATRISTS. *The general hospital management of adult deliberate self-harm: consensus statement on minimum standards for service provision,* 1994.

Chapter 4
Treatment methods and their effectiveness

4.1   This chapter describes ways of helping patients with psychological disorders which can be employed by physicians, with the understanding that a psychiatrist, psychologist or social worker colleague is available for further advice or treatment as necessary. Referral to a psychiatrist is necessary:

- when the physician is faced with a difficult diagnostic problem (eg whether a treatable psychiatric disorder is present in a patient with unexplained physical symptoms or following a stroke);

- when it is unclear whether an antidepressant might benefit a seriously physically ill patient and, if so, which drug to choose;

- when a psychiatric illness has not responded to the physician's treatment (eg antidepressants, or anxiety management);

- when the patient has suicidal ideas;

- when there is an overt management problem (eg suicidal threat, psychotic ideation, non-compliance etc).

4.2   Many patients are upset and offended at the suggestion of referral to a psychiatrist. If, however, the physician has performed a full psychological assessment and even commenced psychiatric treatment, the suggestion that a colleague is being asked to see the patient because of his/her greater expertise is logical and easy to explain to the patient. Some patients have to be specifically reassured that psychiatric referral does not indicate that they are 'mad' or 'hopeless'. The more readily available the psychiatrist and the closer the physician and psychiatrist work together, the easier the referral.

Psychological disorders in the physically ill — adjustment, anxiety and depressive disorders

Adjustment disorders

4.3   *Diagnosis:* The appropriate treatment for an adjustment disorder is to help the patient make a more adaptive response to illness. To do this, the doctor and/or nurse needs to spend time with the patient explaining the illness, its treatment and offering support as necessary. Specialist nurses may be particularly helpful in this task as their specialised knowledge (eg in relation to stomas, prostheses, diabetes) enables them to bring practical as well as emotional support. When an adjustment reaction occurs it should be noted in the discharge summary so that the GP can commence early antidepressant treatment if the symptoms persist or worsen after discharge. Counselling services should be used when appropriate, but only after the patient has been assessed to ensure that he/she does not have a serious psychological disorder that requires specific treatment.

4.4   *Prevention:* There is an opportunity for prevention of adjustment disorders (and possible ensuing depressive disorders) if staff time and effort is devoted to this. For example, in their prospective study of counselling men in a coronary care unit, Thompson and Meddis[101] demonstrated that a structured support and education package given to the patients and their wives while the patients were in hospital significantly reduced scores of anxiety and depression. Following discharge, anxiety was significantly reduced with respect to return to work, leisure activities, sexual activity, and a further heart attack.

Anxiety disorders

4.5   Specific treatment may be required for specific phobias, for example of needles or chemotherapy, or for more generalised anxiety concerning coping with a serious illness such as multiple sclerosis, cancer or diabetes. In each case, psychological treatment is preferable to anxiolytic drugs; the former is largely concerned with explanation and support and can be administered by a physician or nurse. Alternatively the physician can recommend the patient to use a relaxation tape and/or attend yoga or relaxation classes. It is worth remembering that there may be additional problems in the patient's life outside the hospital, such as an ill relative at home, which also require attention.

4.6   When more specialised treatment is required, this is best administered by a psychologist who will employ relaxation (for generalised anxiety/tension), systematic desensitisation (for phobias), biofeedback, cognitive-behavioural therapy or dynamic psychotherapy, according to the nature of the complaint, the patient's personality and the psychologist's own training.

4.7   Certain drugs may be helpful when used for short duration. Brief treatment with benzodiazepines, or low doses of a major tranquilliser such as thioridazine, are helpful for inpatients but it is essential that these drugs be stopped before discharge. Their use for outpatients must also be limited; hospital doctors should confer with the patient's GP before starting such medication, which should be stopped before dependence occurs. Certain somatic symptoms, eg palpitations and tremor, respond well to beta-blockers.

Depressive disorders

4.8   Management of depressive disorders must also be related to the causal factors. Where the depression appears closely bound up with a life-threatening, disabling or near terminal illness, the patient should be encouraged to ventilate worries and problems with a suitable member of staff and should be provided with practical support where possible. Where depression persists at the level of depressive disorder, irrespective of its cause, an antidepressant is indicated.

4.9 Antidepressant medication is effective in the majority of patients and is usually well tolerated. The newer antidepressants are more expensive but can be prescribed for patients who have cardiac disorders, glaucoma and prostatism, in whom tricyclic antidepressants are contraindicated. They can also be used in other patients who develop major side effects on tricyclic antidepressants. There is little difference in efficacy between the different classes of antidepressants — their use is reviewed in detail by Fava.[102] Electroconvulsive therapy (ECT) is an effective treatment for severe depression that does not respond to antidepressants.

4.10 Two reviews indicate the efficacy of antidepressants in general medical patients.[103,104] The main benefit of antidepressants in the medically ill is to double the chance of recovery from depressive illness (from about 30% to 65%). Such recovery may be accompanied by improvement in the physical condition. For example, in stroke patients improvement of depression may be associated with improvement in activities of daily living.[105,106] Antidepressants also have an analgesic effect in addition to their antidepressive effect.[107] Two reviews indicated that in the majority of clinical trials an improvement of up to 55% in the treatment of chronic pain was reported.[107,108]

4.11 Depressive disorders may benefit from cognitive therapy, either as an alternative or as an adjunct to antidepressant medication.[109] This form of therapy tackles directly negative ideas about illness, its disabling effects and prognosis, all of which become exaggerated in depressive disorder. It requires the skilled help of a psychologist or psychiatrist and may be used as an alternative to antidepressant medication in mild depressive disorders. Psychological treatment with cancer patients has been demonstrated to reduce anxiety and depression by approximately 50% compared with controls.[110]

Dementia

4.12 The management of dementia involves:

a practical advice and medical help for carers, if necessary;

b psychological support, including attention to the carer's feelings towards the patient;

c advice about sensitive issues such as when a person with dementia should stop driving;

d providing information about the availability of local medical and social service resources, and also the role of voluntary bodies such as the Alzheimer's Disease Society;

e management of depression accompanying the dementia;

f reality orientation which may be helpful in the early stages;

g advice to the family;

h appropriate use of sedative medication;

i appropriate treatment with newer antidepressants of the depression that can accompany dementia (tricyclic antidepressants should be avoided if possible as their anticholinergic effects may further impair memory function).

Delirium (acute confusional state)

4.13 The management of an acute confusional state involves two separate related strategies. The first is to identify and treat the underlying cause, which will be an infection or drug reaction in most cases, and the second is the management of the state of delirium itself, until it resolves. The latter includes general nursing measures to orient the patient, maintain human contact in a consistent way and, if necessary, judicious use of medication.[19,32,120]

Alcohol misuse

4.14 Counselling by an experienced nurse (in a single session of 60 minutes) of men in a medical ward with problem drinking was shown in one study to lead to a significant improvement in alcohol related problems over the subsequent 12 months, compared with a control group.[84] In this study each patient was given a specially prepared booklet and engaged in a discussion on lifestyle and health, which helped him to weigh up the drawbacks of his pattern of drinking and to come to a decision about his future consumption. Further details of similar interventions are summarised in the *Effective Care Bulletin*.[85]

Medically unexplained symptoms

4.15 If the physician decides that organic disease is unlikely to be the cause of a patient's symptom(s), a management plan is needed which:

a addresses the patient's worries about serious illness and coexisting life problems;

b includes the minimum number of investigations;

c provides an explanation for the symptoms which is acceptable to the patient;

d offers treatment for anxiety or depressive disorders, if present.

Further details on medically unexplained symptoms are given in Appendix B.

4.16 Psychological treatment for medically unexplained symptoms has generally been organised around specific syndromes. Examples include the successful psychological treatment for irritable bowel syndrome,[111] atypical chest pain[112] chronic fatigue syndrome[113] and hypochondriasis.[114] The overall conclusion from the controlled trials is that there was marked improvement in both symptoms and disability in approximately two-thirds of cases compared with a small proportion of control subjects.[115]

4.17   The example of psychological treatments used in the irritable bowel syndrome will illustrate the range of treatments required. For first-time referrals initial treatment in the outpatient department with stress management may be more effective than routine medical treatment in the long term. Rumsey and colleagues treated patients in groups of eight; there were six weekly sessions of 1.5 hours each conducted by a clinical psychologist (the gastroenterologist and dietitian participated in one session).[139] Patients treated in these groups improved significantly more than those treated pharmacologically; the latter made only a short-term improvement with symptoms returning to pre-treatment levels by six months. 'Refractory' irritable bowel syndrome demands much more intensive psychological treatment with detailed psychological assessment and management on an individual or group basis.[111,116,117]

Chronic, multiple unexplained symptoms

4.18   Chronic, multiple unexplained symptoms present a difficult clinical problem. Doctors who try to achieve great changes with patients who have chronic, multiple unexplained symptoms are often disappointed; a conservative management policy, which reduces both disability and the use of expensive investigation, is preferred. Once such patients are identified they should be seen regularly, but not necessarily frequently, by the same *senior* doctor, who can accept the patient's symptomatology and disability without recourse to repeated investigations and be prepared to provide supportive interviews instead; these are often best held with the spouse present so that the doctor's tolerant and encouraging stance can be adopted by the relative, who otherwise feels the only course of action is to press for further opinions, tests and treatments. It has been shown that care by a single doctor, who reviews the patient every three months and resists the patient's requests for further investigations, especially those performed as an inpatient, can reduce the cost.[118] Continued care and decisions regarding any possible further investigations should not be left to junior medical staff.

4.19   Because management of these symptoms can be so difficult, general preventive measures should be employed whenever possible. They should be used for all somatising patients, preferably before the complaints have become chronic and disabling. As soon as it is clear that symptoms cannot be medically explained, eg when investigations such as gastrointestinal endoscopy or a coronary angiogram are normal, explanation of the probable underlying mechanisms and reattribution (see Appendix B) may prevent the symptoms becoming chronic. All doctors must be careful to avoid prescribing inappropriate medication (eg powerful analgesia) or performing investigations that are not truly clinically indicated even if the patient puts some pressure on the doctor to do so.[119]

4.20   The rehabilitation of patients with chronic somatisation is difficult and can generally be undertaken only at specialised units, unless the patient and his/her relatives are unusually well motivated. Such rehabilitation usually includes the help of a psychologist or a psychiatrist working closely with the medical team, as occurs in a pain clinic. Modification of the patients's problematic illness behaviour and an increase in general activities often require intensive inpatient treatment. An example of such treatment is the pain clinic (para 6.33). The outcome of treatment in pain clinics depends on the patients taken on for treatment. Some clinics focus almost entirely on pain associated with malignancy, while others see substantial numbers of patients whose pain dates from a work injury. In addition, some apply stringent criteria to the selection of patients for treatment (for example, not accepting any involved in litigation), while others accept most patients who are referred. One report[144] suggested that 42% of 485 patients treated in a pain clinic gained complete or partial relief from their pain. A meta-analysis of 65 reports of multi-modal treatment of chronic back pain[145] suggests that, overall, treatment groups improved 30% more than control groups in the short term and 38% more in the longer term (average of two years). Outcome was superior on a wide range of measures including pain behaviour, activity, use of medication and health services, and return to work.

4.21 Referral of a patient with chronic somatisation to a psychiatrist or psychologist to assess whether any form of psychological therapy might be effective is worthwhile, provided the physician has a good working relationship with the psychiatrist (otherwise the patient is unlikely to be prepared to see the psychiatrist). The physician should resist any tendency to refer on to other medical specialists as this tends to perpetuate the endless search for causes or specific treatments.

Deliberate self-harm

4.22 The psychological management of deliberate self-harm patients may begin with acute problems of behaviour in the medical ward, especially if the patient resists necessary treatment for the self-harm or insists on immediate discharge. This requires immediate assessment from the liaison psychiatric team, especially if detention under the Mental Health Act is being considered. Later management involves thorough assessment of the reasons for the deliberate self-harm and help for the underlying problem, which may be social, behavioural or psychiatric. Evidence for the efficacy of the various forms of assessment has been reviewed;[65] it is difficult to evaluate. Since the overall repetition rate is low (approximately 15% over the following year), very large studies would be required to demonstrate the superiority of one type of assessment *in terms of repetition rate*; to date no studies of this size have been conducted. Existing evidence demonstrates that brief problem-solving counselling by a nurse or psychologist, task-centred social work by a social worker or assessment and treatment by a psychiatrist leads to significant improvement in social problems and psychiatric symptoms.[65]

Sexual, relationship and body image problems, and eating disorders

4.23   Sexual and relationship problems are responsive to psychological treatment, usually marital therapy or counselling with a partner.[69] Clarification of the problem followed by education and advice is sometimes all that is needed. Specific psychological treatment which reduces anxiety that accompanies increasing sexual arousal may be appropriate (see Further Reading).

4.24   Body image problems are usually responsive to behavioural therapy. This involves learning the technique of progressive muscular relaxation and applying this procedure while discussing and viewing the affected part; alternatively, cognitive therapy may be used to challenge the irrational beliefs which many patients develop, such as the assumption that they will be rejected by their partner because of the bodily change. For some body image problems there may be a place for surgical reconstruction.

4.25   Management of eating disorders involves behavioural therapy techniques to restore a normal eating pattern and weight. Such treatment may have to be in a psychiatric ward if there is severe weight loss. Individual and family psychotherapy are often required; drugs rarely have a major role in management unless the patient has a depressive disorder. The patient with anorexia and concurrent diabetes requires special care, as does the suicidal patient; very occasionally it is necessary to detain the patient under a section of the Mental Health Act. Such difficult management situations require the closest working together of medical, nursing and psychiatric staff: a specialised unit that can offer simultaneous psychological and physical care (liaison inpatient unit) is desirable.

Chapter 4
Summary and recommendations

Evidence exists to support the efficacy of antidepressants and psychological treatment for the psychological disorders that accompany physical illness and for medically unexplained symptoms (paras 4.10, 4.16). Currently these are underused. It is therefore recommended that:

- All staff should have a basic understanding of the treatment of adjustment disorders, anxiety, depression, dementia and delirium. Physicians should be familiar with the frequently used antidepressants and the correct doses (see Appendix D).

- A counselling service for alcohol problems should be readily available for both inpatients and outpatients (para 4.14).

- Psychological treatment should be considered for patients who have medically unexplained somatic symptoms. If such treatment is necessary it should be available either in primary care or in the general hospital as appropriate. Such treatment should start in the hospital clinic with a positive explanation of the cause of the symptoms; simply sending a report to the GP stating that 'no organic disease is present' is inadequate (para 4.15).

- Patients with chronic multiple symptoms require a specific management plan, involving regular (but not necessarily frequent) appointments with a senior doctor and a minimum number of investigations. Hospital admission should be avoided as far as possible (para 4.18).

- All staff should understand when referral to a psychiatric service is necessary and how this may be negotiated with the patient (paras 4.1, 4.2).

- Adequate audit is essential to demonstrate to purchasers that these aspects of clinical management are appropriately maintained.

Further Reading

SHARPE M, PEVELER R, MAYOU R. The psychological treatment of patients with functional somatic symptoms: a practical guide. *Journal of Psychosomatic Research* 1992;**36:** 515–9.

GOLDBERG DP, BENJAMIN S, CREED F. *Psychiatry in medical practice*, 2nd edn. London, New York: Routledge, 1994: 279–83.

PEARCE S, WARDLE J, eds. *The practice of behavioural medicine.* Oxford Science Publications; British Psychological Society, Oxford University Press, 1989.

TUNKS E, BELLISSIMO A. *Behavioural medicine: concepts and procedures.* Oxford: Pergamon, 1991.

Cost effectiveness of a liaison psychiatry service

The potential for reducing costs

5.1   There are several reasons why an effective liaison psychiatry service may be cost effective. Length of stay in a general hospital ward is increased for patients with psychiatric disorders.[46,121-123] This increase is accounted for partly by the seriousness of the physical illness, but also by cognitive impairment which leads to difficulties in subsequent placement, and by anxiety and depressive disorders which increase pain and disability, reduce recovery rate and delay discharge.[124-126] The potential for reducing the length of stay, and therefore the costs, by better recognition and management of psychological disorders is therefore considerable.

5.2   Outpatient attendances are more numerous in patients with depression and somatisation; in fact, depression is a better predictor of outpatient attendances than the nature of the physical illness.[127,128] Depression in this context also leads to increased pain, disability and problematic illness behaviour. Studies that have demonstrated improved symptoms and disability in patients with medically unexplained symptoms (para 4.16) have not included a cost analysis, but have generally shown a reduction in the number of outpatient visits.

5.3   Alcohol misuse, either alone or in combination with other psychiatric disorders, is associated with greater use of hospital resources even when the primary physical pathology is severe.[129] Eating disorders, especially in conjunction with organic disorders such as renal failure or diabetes, can lead to repeated emergency admissions. Recognition and treatment of these psychiatric disorders may therefore reduce health care utilisation and costs (see para 5.9).

Experimental studies

5.4   The literature on the cost effectiveness of liaison psychiatry in the UK remains very limited. Many of the studies have been performed in the USA, where the health care system is different, so cost data cannot necessarily be translated to the UK. There is a need for more studies based on UK data of the kind described below.

5.5   Several studies have examined the effect on length of stay of introducing a liaison psychiatry service. One example concerned elderly patients with hip fractures.[130] This demonstrated that routine screening at admission of every patient by a psychiatrist, together with appropriate treatment and advice about discharge arrangements, where necessary, led to earlier discharge by two days, saving approximately $260,000 on the costs of treating 452 patients. These savings from the reduction in bed usage were far in excess of the costs of the intervention, the so-called cost-offset effect, so the liaison psychiatry service more than paid for itself. The study demonstrated that the liaison psychiatry service led to a significant reduction of psychiatric symptoms prior to discharge, and shorter periods of rehabilitation were required after discharge from hospital.

5.6   In their meta-analysis of 22 random allocation studies, Mumford *et al*[131] found that psychological interventions for inpatients shortened hospital stay on average by 1.5 days. In a parallel analysis of insurance claims, patients who had received psychiatric care needed significantly less general medical inpatient care than a group without psychiatric care; both groups had similar outpatient care costs. In this study the psychiatric outpatient care was thought to be responsible for reducing the repeated hospitalisations that occurred in the comparison group. A similar conclusion was drawn by Jones and Vischi[129] from their review of 25 different studies where medical service utilisation was used as an outcome measure for psychiatric interventions, and by Mumford *et al* in their review of 13 studies examining the effect of psychiatric intervention after surgery or heart attack.

5.7   In the case of patients who have chronic somatisation, one of the main costs is that of repeated investigations. Smith *et al*[118] demonstrated the efficacy of a single consultation with a psychiatrist for chronic somatisation patients in a large hospital. The psychiatrist wrote a detailed report about psychiatric diagnosis and suggested management which involved regular scheduled appointments with the physician but with an attempt to avoid hospitalisation, diagnostic procedures, laboratory assessments and surgery. There were considerable cost savings as a result of this intervention: the average quarterly cost of all health care fell from $2,681 to $1,606. The reduction in total health care charges in this study was due primarily to a reduction of inpatient care.

Cost effectiveness of pain programmes

5.8   Some of the most detailed cost analyses have concerned the costs and benefits of pain programmes. In one recent study,[133] improvements with outpatient and inpatient treatment programmes were similar at the end of treatment and also 9–18 months later, in respect of measures of pain activity, return to work and appropriate use of medication. At the later follow-up, however, the inpatient group was functioning better than the outpatients, whilst a non-treatment control group had deteriorated. Treatment for inpatients costs seven times more per patient than that for outpatients. Overall cost analysis included savings in accident compensation and sickness benefits (but excluding additional savings in health service costs) for those who had returned to work; when calculated over one year, the outpatient programme showed a gain, the inpatient programme a small deficit. Calculated over five years, however, assuming that the benefits of treatment are sustained, both programmes will result in substantial savings, the inpatient programme saving twice as much as the outpatient treatment.

Alcohol misuse

5.9   The intervention in cases of alcohol misuse described in the previous chapter (para 4.14) is estimated to cost less than £50 in staff time and the cost of the booklet; the saving in reduced medical care, especially if less drinking leads to fewer inpatient admissions, is likely to be far greater than this.[132]

Chapter 5
Summary and recommendations

1   Undetected psychiatric disorder may lead to delayed hospital discharge and excessive investigations, which increase health care costs (para 5.1). Better detection and management of psychological disorders carries the potential to reduce health care costs; there is limited evidence to indicate that the costs saved are many times greater than the cost of the liaison service (para 5.5).

2   It is recommended that further research be performed so that the cost-offset effect of liaison psychiatry services in the UK may be accurately assessed. Specific information is required to discover which interventions are most cost-effective for which groups of patients.

3   Any audit of a liaison psychiatry service should, where possible and appropriate, include some measure of cost savings, as well as measuring quality of service.

Further Reading

HAMMER JS. The cost-benefit of psychiatric consultation/liaison services in the medical setting. *Current Opinion in Psychiatry* 1990; **3**:687–91.

BENJAMIN S, BRIDGES K. The need for specialist services for chronic somatisers. In: Benjamin S, House A, Jenkins P, eds. *Liaison psychiatry: defining needs and planning services*. London: Gaskell, 1994: 16–23.

Chapter 6
Models of liaison psychiatric services

Introduction

6.1　This chapter describes different models of liaison services. The first section, which describes a generic liaison psychiatry team, is followed by examples of the direct consultation, specialist nurse and liaison models. These are not intended to be specific to any particular specialty — any model might be appropriate for any specialty depending on local circumstances and preference.

A generic liaison psychiatric team

6.2　A liaison psychiatry team would typically include:

- a full-time liaison psychiatrist (consultant);

- one or more training psychiatrists (at registrar or senior registrar grade);

- two clinical nurse specialists;

- a social worker; and

- a clinical psychologist who should be a member of the team or attached to it.

6.3　The inpatient referrals to a liaison team from medical and surgical wards over a 12-month period are illustrated in the first column of Table 6.1; deliberate self-harm and psychiatric disorders associated with physical illness predominate.[167] Liaison services including both inpatient and outpatient referrals to a consultant-led liaison service (excluding deliberate self-harm patients and other patients seen by junior psychiatric staff) show similar proportions of patients with medically unexplained symptoms and psychiatric disorders associated with physical disease. For each of these groups the referred patients represent only a tiny minority of all patients with such symptoms in the hospital.[42] The table gives some indication of the morbidity that is referred to an established, but limited, liaison service. It demonstrates the importance of having a full liaison service, not just one that assesses deliberate self-harm patients. There are data to show that an increasingly active liaison psychiatric service increases referrals of patients with medically unexplained symptoms and psychological disorders associated with physical illness;[134,135] the numbers of patients referred to the liaison service will therefore grow considerably as liaison services develop.

Liaison psychiatrist

6.4　The work of the liaison psychiatrist in such a team includes:

- Providing a *consultation service* to physicians and surgeons, who retain responsibility for their patients. This may be a 'one off' consultation or may involve

Table 6.1
Percentage of inpatients and outpatients with psychological disorders who were referred to liaison psychiatry services covering inpatients (first column) and those covering inpatients and outpatients (right hand columns). Data taken from references 7, 47,167.

Disorder	Inpatients		Inpatients and outpatients combined	Inpatients and outpatients separately	
	Oxford (*n* = 418)	Leicester (*n* = 468)	Leicester (*n* = 300)	Manchester (*n* = 279)	
	%	%	%	%	
				Inpatients (*n* = 120)	Outpatients (*n* = 159)
1 Psychological disorder and physical illness	42	29	32	32	26
2 Medically unexplained symptoms	12	9	30	28	45
3 Drug and alcohol abuse	2	4	15	11	3
4 Deliberate self-harm	33	48	NA	NA	NA
5 Dementia and delirium	6	8	13	12	1
6 Miscellaneous, including eating disorders	5	2	10	17	25

supervising psychiatric treatment while the patient remains on a medical/surgical ward.

■ Taking over *clinical responsibility* for patients referred by physicians and surgeons for outpatient or inpatient psychiatric treatment (a few hospitals have liaison beds, usually as a separate ward). Approximately half the referred patients require continued care from the psychiatrist, usually as outpatients. Approximately 14% of referrals require inpatient psychiatric treatment.[7,47]

■ Providing a *liaison service* to particular units, for example weekly meetings with renal, intensive care or bone marrow transplant units.

Clinical nurse specialist

6.5 The work of the clinical nurse specialists in the liaison team commonly involves individual work with patients, such as the assessment and treatment of deliberate self-harm patients. The nurse may develop special expertise in the management of problems concerning alcohol and drug misuse, sexual abuse, or adolescents, which leads to referrals from all departments of the general hospital. Some clinical nurse specialists may work solely or primarily on specific units such as accident and emergency, oncology, cardiac or AIDS units. The liaison nurses also have a very important supportive role to nursing staff on general and medical wards. This role includes:

- Giving advice, guidance and support to nurses working in the general wards and A&E departments regarding the care of patients with psychological problems.

- Advising on the management and nursing care of patients who exhibit suicidal tendencies or disturbed and violent behaviour.

- Advising nursing and junior medical staff on the care of patients admitted following self-harm, including care while on the medical ward and recommendations for follow-up that includes other agencies such as social services, Alcoholics Anonymous, voluntary agencies.

- Giving advice and support to midwives in the obstetric unit on the care of mothers with actual or potential psychological problems.

- Providing advice and support to staff within the accident and emergency department on how to handle psychiatric emergencies and effect smooth transfer to the psychiatric unit.

- Having discussions with local police and other agencies in the community who are involved in psychiatric emergencies.

6.6 *General nurses* often talk at length to patients; they also already use a comprehensive assessment process. This means that they have many opportunities to be involved in identifying psychological problems, including understanding how a patient's personal difficulties, not often disclosed to the doctors, may exacerbate the pain and distress of physical illness or lead to somatisation. Recognition and management of the latter would be greatly enhanced if nurses could be trained to carry out brief, focused interviews for psychological disorders (see Appendix C) with all inpatients and outpatients being investigated for the common physical symptoms that are often medically unexplained, eg atypical chest pain, abdominal pain, chronic fatigue. If the list of investigations included a psychosocial assessment, performed by either nurse or doctor, the results of these brief interviews could be collated and the appropriate treatment initiated in the hospital, or the details specified in the letter to the GP.

Psychiatric social worker

6.7 The psychiatric social worker performs individual patient assessments but will often also be involved in a regular medical-psychosocial case conference, which includes the physicians, nursing and other staff who work on a single unit and, sometimes, the liaison psychiatrist.[136] The discussion may involve a single patient who is presenting a particular management problem, or a number of patients; in either case the information provided from sources outside the hospital will give a more complete picture of the patient's home environment and lead to a better management plan. The social worker may relay information from other sources and/or invite to the meeting a hostel warden, a local priest or others who work with the patient in the community. The social worker may also have special expertise in working with the patient's family.

Clinical psychologist

6.8 The clinical psychologist has skills that are relevant to many of the psychological problems seen in the general hospital and, like those of other liaison team members, often urgently required. For this reason it is more satisfactory to have a clinical psychologist with a specific attachment to the liaison team than a psychologist based in the community or other mental health setting, to whom the patient might be referred. Examples of treatments that are typically performed by a psychologist are:

- Desensitisation to phobias of needles, dialysis or chemotherapy

- Anxiety management for somatic symptoms related to anxiety, such as headaches, chest pain, breathlessness, diarrhoea

- Cognitive therapy for depression, which might relieve medically unexplained symptoms and/or facilitate 'coping' with severe organic disease

- Treatment of sexual disorders by sensate focusing

- Behavioural treatment of chronic pain

- Cognitive assessment of patients with suspected brain damage

- Biofeedback, eg for headache

- Advice on managing troublesome or antisocial behaviour in the general ward.

Method of working

6.9 The liaison team may operate in several ways. Patients may be referred to a central referral point (eg liaison team secretary/administrator) and the consultant liaison psychiatrist will decide which member of the team will assess and treat a particular patient; alternatively, the referral may go direct to the member of the liaison team who has most expertise in the area of concern. In some hospitals there are several consultant psychiatrists who take liaison referrals and the physician will usually refer to the psychiatrist with whom he/she has a strong working relationship. In other hospitals individual psychologists have developed particular working relationships with particular units, such as neurology, palliative care, renal medicine, and the pain clinic.

The direct consultation model

6.10 Direct consultation models have been described in those specialties where many patients have medically unexplained symptoms (eg gastroenterology and neurology). Approximately half such patients have psychiatric disorders[29] and, in view of the large numbers, it is neither feasible nor desirable that they should all be referred to a psychiatrist or a psychologist. Many will receive help from a GP or from a hospital doctor who will feel more confident to manage these patients if he/she receives support from the liaison psychiatrist.[2,137]

Psychiatrist or psychologist in the clinic

6.11 In order that the physician can provide psychological care, and to facilitate referral to the psychiatrist when appropriate, it is necessary to have ready access to psychiatric advice. One way this has been achieved is by having a psychiatrist within the medical clinic who can offer an immediate opinion and to whom a patient can be introduced when a referral is made. This means that the patient can be taken by the physician to another room in the same clinic and be introduced in person, rather than be asked to accept a referral to the psychiatric clinic at a later date — a prospect that can fill many people with horror because of the fears and fantasies that such a suggestion may provoke.[138]

Combined clinic

6.12 An alternative arrangement is to establish a combined clinic. This is a well established practice in the care of elderly people (geriatrician with an old age psychiatrist) and is also a highly desirable way of delivering optimal care for patients with unexplained physical symptoms, for which the combined opinions of a physician and a psychiatrist are often necessary. An example of a combined clinic is a chronic fatigue clinic. These clinics are now held in several centres around the UK and enable necessary physical and psychological investigations to be performed together without discussion of whether the disorder is 'physical' or 'psychological'.

Direct referral to group psychological treatment

6.13 A further example of a direct consultation model would be the development of a group, led by a psychologist, to whom patients with a particular condition, eg irritable bowel syndrome (IBS)[139] may be referred. Such group psychological treatment might typically involve six weekly sessions at which the following topics could be discussed: the nature of IBS, the role of stress in IBS, progressive muscle relaxation and its regular usage, diet and fitness, problem solving and long-term management of IBS.

6.14 Patient satisfaction with psychological treatment and its successful long-term outcome suggests it should be more widely available, in the form of individual or group treatment.[140]

The specialist nurse model

6.15 Since their attention is focused on the physical aspects of treatment of diseases such as cancer, medical and nursing staff tend to overlook psychiatric disorders. For this reason the traditional consultation service, which relies on clinicians making referrals to psychiatrists, would refer only a small proportion of those cancer patients needing psychological help, so specialist cancer nurses have been trained to detect psychiatric disorders in some units. The model is applicable to other units with specialised nurses, eg diabetic clinics.

The role of specialist cancer nurses

6.16 The training of specialist cancer nurses involves developing the appropriate psychological assessment skills, helping to relinquish distancing strategies which inhibit patient disclosure, and learning the necessary referral criteria. This enables them to assess and accurately recognise over 90% of those patients who need psychological or psychiatric help.[141] To maintain this recognition rate, specialist nurses also need regular supervision and prompt psychological and psychiatric specialist help when requested.

6.17 The specialist nurse scheme is labour intensive if all patients are followed up regardless of whether they are coping with their illness or not. Some patients, who are coping satisfactorily, would prefer to put things to the back of their minds; regular review would lead only to unnecessary increased worry. It is therefore preferable to use a more targeted approach in which specialist nurses see all patients in the hospital but limit further contact to one home visit unless the patient has psychological problems. The patient is invited to make further contact with the nurse if problems develop later. This limited intervention has been found to be as effective as the full intervention[142] and carries the additional advantage that the specialist nurses are not faced with an accumulating load of patients who really do not need their help.

6.18 The services of the specialist cancer nurse would be even more effective if patients at particular risk of developing psychiatric morbidity could be identified early. Some useful markers have now been established which include: a past history of psychiatric illness, a perception that the information given about illness and treatment was inadequate, and the number of unresolved concerns about the disease or treatment. Patients fitting these categories are monitored within the first few months of diagnosis and attempts made to help them resolve their concerns.

The liaison team and its evaluation

6.19 At one large cancer hospital the liaison psychiatric service consists of two consultant psychiatrists, a research registrar, a rotating registrar and a clinical psychologist. Referrals are made to the team via the specialist nurses, and also by the physicians, their junior staff and general nursing staff. Each referral is phoned through and recorded on a standard form and allocated to a particular psychiatrist or psychologist. This allows prompt action to be taken. The referring person later receives a report by letter or telephone. This scheme now deals with some four to five hundred patients a year.

6.20 Regular audit meetings are held to monitor the pattern of service and to discuss difficult cases. A critical aspect of the liaison service has been continual attempts to evaluate its impact on the level of psychiatric, psychological and social morbidity in cancer patients and their relatives. It has been established that a monitoring system based on the specialist nurses, combined with other referrals, is effective in producing a four-fold reduction in ongoing psychiatric morbidity.[89]

Advantages and disadvantages

6.21   The role of specialist nurses can be expanded as their skills develop to include coun-selling and specific behavioural techniques such as training in anxiety management and cognitive therapy. This means that direct treatment for many of the patients' dif-ficulties can be offered without referral to the liaison team.

6.22   However, the use of specialist nurses without proper supervision and team working carries certain dangers. First, the specialist nurse can come to be seen as the person solely responsible for psychological care and this then allows clinicians and other health professionals to opt out of this aspect of treatment. Second, nurses who do not have supervision tend to revert to former interview styles with distancing strate-gies, particularly if prompt psychological and psychiatric back-up is not available to them. Third, there is also a danger that such a specialist team will try to take over the psychological care of all cancer patients instead of co-ordinating their input with the patient's own general practitioner who will usually wish to be involved in this aspect of care. To avoid this, the specialist nurses are asked to discuss with general practitioners the appropriateness of psychological or psychiatric referral before ini-tiating it.

6.23   A longer term aim is to upgrade the skills of *all* health professionals who work in a general hospital in order that they become better able to recognise patients who need psychological and psychiatric help. Pilot studies have shown that this is possi-ble and that clinicians can begin to take on first-line treatment themselves before considering referral. This means that the scheme is becoming increasingly efficient and effective by spreading the load of psychological care.

The liaison model

6.24   The liaison model has been used successfully in an alcohol service, as described here, but may also be used in any unit where the staff need support because of the demanding nature of the clinical work (see para 6.32). The central event of the alco-hol service is a weekly liaison meeting that usually lasts no more than one hour. This meeting is attended by the physicians (senior and junior), the psychiatrist, psychi-atric nurses and social work staff as well as by staff working in local alcohol hostels and with the Council on Addiction. The participating agencies chair the meeting in turn. Patients are never seen at this meeting; its functions include discussion of referrals and their appropriate treatment, and issues of education and training. The meetings foster development and maintenance of mutual trust, vital in a field where negative sentiments may develop only too readily and interfere with patient care.

6.25   Each meeting includes a brief educational presentation on such topics as the use of beta-blockers, cost/benefit analysis of various alcohol services, family violence and sexual abuse. Discussion of a particular patient or group of patients identifies gaps or failures in the combined services and this can lead to joint enterprises for their solution. Working closely together in this way, members of the group attending the meeting extend their understanding of the medical and psychological problems of substance misusers.

6.26   While it might be thought that much of the work done in a meeting such as this could be done over the telephone, regular face-to-face contact between staff from such disparate working settings makes all subsequent contact by telephone and letter both easier and more efficient. Alcohol misusers often induce powerful negative feelings in those who try to help them. This is so for physicians who have to treat repeated episodes of liver failure, or other physical complications of alcohol misuse, knowing that the person continues to misuse alcohol, and for the psychiatric team whose therapeutic efforts may meet with disappointments and failures. It is therefore important to have a meeting where these feelings can be openly expressed, and where realistic expectations and achievable goals of management can be established.

6.27   The meeting allows consensus about treatment philosophy in general as well as in relation to particular patients. A treatment philosophy implies a set of shared ideas about the patient's motivation to change his or her drinking pattern; patients are informed of the causes and consequences of their drinking and told explicitly that it is their own responsibility to decide whether to take up any treatment offered. The communication established through the meeting allows all those involved in the care of alcohol misusers to adopt a similar set of expectations and to feel supported when risky decisions are made.

Advantages of the liaison model

6.28   *Rapid and complete referrals:* Many alcohol misusers who are referred by a physician fail to attend their appointment with a psychiatrist; this is wasteful of time and resources and frustrating for both sets of staff. Close liaison leads to good communication and the development of strategies which lead to a high proportion of successful referrals.

6.29   *Helping staff to cope with the stress of care:* Physicians and nurses find dealing with the disturbed behaviour patterns of some patients with alcohol problems to be stressful and such behaviour may also disrupt the medical inpatient service especially if it is not correctly handled. Working closely with psychiatric colleagues can assist the physician in the prevention and management of troublesome behaviour. Psychiatrists too find people with alcohol problems stressful to care for, because of the high rate of relapse and because of physical complications, which are difficult to manage if there is no easy access to diagnostic and treatment facilities: close liaison with the physicians means such facilities are much more readily available. Many staff report greater work satisfaction in a comprehensive system of care which includes both physical and psychological elements and which can respond to all the major needs of the patient.

6.30   *Co-operation with GPs:* Many people with alcohol problems have so damaged their relationships with their GPs that co-operation in management has been withdrawn. Furthermore, some patients have no fixed abode and no GP. A close liaison service can temporarily remedy these disadvantages until relationships with the GP have been established or repaired.

6.31 *Development of services and economic advantages:* Physicians and psychiatrists working together to develop alcohol services can be a great deal more persuasive to commissioning agents and provider units than either can be alone. Liaison schemes, as stated earlier, can help to reduce the length of stay on medical wards and also avoid the long wait for transfer that otherwise often occurs. Furthermore, the availability of the psychiatric day services and acute hostel places enables many patients to avoid admission to both psychiatric and medical beds. Evidence for the effectiveness of specific alcohol treatment has recently been published.[132]

The liaison model in other medical units

6.32 Although the liaison model has been described in relation to a service for people with alcohol problems, the model is equally applicable to other high stress areas of medical practice where staff work closely with patients whose illness may often fail to respond to intensive therapeutic efforts. Examples include intensive care, renal dialysis and bone marrow transplant units, where the opportunity for medical, nursing and social work staff to meet and discuss their feelings about patients may help the unit operate more satisfactorily.[143]

Multidisciplinary assessment model

6.33 An example of a multidisciplinary assessment model is the pain clinic. Such clinics vary in their emphasis and approach. Early clinics, while recognising the importance of psychosocial aspects of pain, tended to be concerned largely with anaesthetic and surgical methods of pain relief. However, the importance of psychological and personality factors in chronic pain has become increasingly recognised, and with this has evolved the establishment of clinics and inpatient units which concentrate on modifying pain-related behaviour as part of a multi-modal approach. Similar recognition of the importance of physical and psychological aspects in, for example, diabetic care is leading to the development of similar multidisciplinary teams for other groups of patients.

6.34 Pain clinics can be grouped into:

a   those where the primary emphasis is medico-surgical;

b   those where no surgery is performed and where the emphasis is on psychiatric and psychological aspects of the patient's pain; and

c   clinics which seek to integrate both approaches. The staff of the last type of clinic will include a psychiatrist, neurosurgeon, physician, anaesthetist, nurse, neurologist, social worker and physiotherapist. Treatments employed include nerve blocks, pharmacotherapy (analgesics, antidepressants and other psychotropic drugs), biofeedback, assisted relaxation training and psychotherapy.

6.35 The multidisciplinary team represents a model that might be adapted to run clinics for medically unexplained symptoms, eg chronic fatigue. The range of disciplines means that psychological, social and physical aspects of a patient's complaint can be evaluated simultaneously.

Multidisciplinary hospital clinical meetings

6.36 Many of the key elements of these joint working practices can be developed if the liaison psychiatric team is invited to present cases at multidisciplinary hospital clinical meetings. As well as being an educational occasion, this forum allows and encourages open discussion between physicians and psychiatrists about difficult cases and can clarify when referral to the liaison team is beneficial and appropriate.[7] This is a cost-effective way of developing the 'liaison' aspect of the consultation model (para 1.10).

Chapter 6
Summary and recommendations

As a liaison team is developed the number of referrals increases. It is only when a reasonable service is developed that patients with psychological disorders associated with physical illness and medically unexplained symptoms reach the psychiatric service in any numbers (para 6.3). This chapter describes a basic liaison team and a variety of models, which may be used with specific medical hospital departments. It is recommended that:

- All hospitals need a consultant-led liaison psychiatry service as a basis for meeting the mental health needs of their patients (para 6.4).

- Every provider unit should consider which model of liaison psychiatry is locally appropriate and agree this with the purchaser as described in the *Health of the Nation* key area handbook (paras 6.12, 6.13, 6.24, 6.33).

- Large hospitals may need to provide a range of liaison psychiatry services to meet the needs of the patients on different medical units.

Further Reading

BENJAMIN S, HOUSE A, JENKINS P, eds. *Liaison psychiatry: defining needs and planning services.* London: Gaskell Press, 1994.

Chapter 4 — EGAN-MORRISS E, MORRISS R, HOUSE A. The role of the nurse in consultation-liaison psychiatry. pp 34–46.

Chapter 5 — BLEWETT A, JENKINS P. Setting up a consultation-liaison psychiatry service in South Gwent. pp 47–57.

Chapter 6 — HOUSE A. Liaison psychiatry in a large teaching hospital: the service at Leeds General Infirmary. pp 58–64.

Chapter 7 — MAGUIRE P, HOPWOOD P. Providing a psychiatric service to a large cancer hospital. pp 65–9.

Chapter 7
Liaison psychiatry service: provision and purchasing

The main points of this document relevant to purchasers are included as Appendix G. For ease of access by commissioners of services this is being published as a separate document *The psychological care of medical patients: recognition and service provision — a guide for purchasers.*

Extent of the need

7.1 The extent of the mental health needs of patients in a general hospital was reviewed in Chapter 2. Anxiety and depressive disorders occur in approximately 15% of patients with organic disease and up to half of patients with medically unexplained symptoms. Alcohol problems, deliberate self-harm and dementia are all primarily psychiatric problems which are frequently found in the general hospital. Eating disorders are much less common but can cause serious problems of management if they coexist with such organic disorders as diabetes. Psychological problems are found throughout all clinical departments (eg obstetrics and gynaecology, ENT, general surgery) and are not confined to patients under the care of physicians. The majority of these mental health problems are similar in severity to those seen by general practitioners and it should be within the remit of hospital doctors to detect them and provide appropriate treatment.

7.2 The accident and emergency (A&E) department of a general hospital is often the first place where medical help is sought for psychiatric problems. The proportion of A&E attenders with psychiatric problems is, of course, greatly increased if the A&E department is a 'place of safety' under the 1983 Mental Health Act; this is frequently but not always the case. Even when primary psychiatric emergencies are received elsewhere, up to about 5% of A&E attenders will have purely psychiatric problems, while 20–30% will have significant psychiatric symptoms coexisting with physical disorder. The A&E department of a district general hospital serving a population of 400,000 may annually expect to receive 800 patients following deliberate self-harm.

7.3 The extent of mental health needs in the medical departments is such that they can be met only by (a) improved management of mental health problems by physicians and nurses on medical units and in A&E departments, and (b) the availability of specialist liaison psychiatry services. This chapter concerns the latter.

Location of the service

7.4 It is essential that the psychiatric services dealing with mental health needs of medical patients be based in the general hospital. There are several reasons for this:

a   Problems may be so acute that they can be dealt with only by a psychiatrist on site (eg acutely disturbed patients on a medical ward, assessment of some deliberate self-harm patients, especially those threatening to leave hospital, and psychiatric emergencies in A&E).

b   Patients with chronic and multiple unexplained symptoms may not attend the psychiatric department in spite of clear underlying psychiatric disorder.

c   Physical illness, especially if chronic, may require the patient to attend the general hospital so often that additional visits elsewhere to deal with concurrent psychiatric difficulties would be unjustified (eg disabling neurological illness and depression, cancer and body image problems).

d   Psychiatric and physical disorders may be so intimately linked that effective psychiatric care can only be delivered when integrated with physical care (eg eating disorders and diabetes; mood disturbance and renal dialysis).

e   General psychiatric services are increasingly community-based and geographically defined; it can become exceedingly inefficient for psychiatrists to travel from elsewhere to see patients in the general hospital.

f   Liaison psychiatric services are often best developed by psychiatrists whose major commitment is to this work. Liaison work cannot be done well if it is seen as an extra duty distracting from the central functions of community-based general services.

7.5   It must be recognised that an important route for approximately a quarter of all new patients entering the psychiatric service is via the general hospital;[77] no mental health service can afford to ignore this important route to treatment.

Components of the service

7.6   The liaison psychiatric service should have the following components:

a   A range of psychiatric, psychological, nursing and social work skills in order to advise other staff in the hospital and treat patients as appropriate.

b   An A&E psychiatry service available for advice 24 hours a day, seven days a week. Psychiatrists should be available quickly to attend busy A&E departments, for example in inner city areas where psychiatric emergencies and other primary psychiatric problems are common.

c   An emergency liaison service to deal with psychiatric emergencies elsewhere in the general hospital.

d   Liaison psychiatric services to particular medical and surgical departments, including their inpatient and outpatient elements.

(Geographically defined psychiatric services, which may have general hospital elements, and old age and child psychiatric services, are not considered here.)

7.7 The extent of liaison psychiatric services varies greatly from place to place, depending among other things on case mix and physician-psychiatrist relationships, interests and skills. Adequate liaison inpatient accommodation is particularly important and should be separate from general psychiatric catchment beds, because the types of patient needing 'liaison' and 'general' admission are very different.

7.8 Liaison psychiatric work involves detailed personal interviews which should be unhurried and conducted in quiet, comfortable and safe surroundings where confidentiality can be assured. Adequate space in A&E and other departments is essential. Immediate access to translation and interpretation services is needed for people from ethnic minorities.

Personnel

Deployment and number of staff

7.9 Psychiatric interviewing, assessment and treatment are time-consuming activities; it is impossible to provide an adequate liaison psychiatric service without adequate staff who can devote sufficient time for their work to be carried out properly. As a general guide, an initial interview may often require up to an hour; in addition, the psychiatrist has to spend further time examining notes and talking to staff and relatives. Subsequent interviews take between 30 and 60 minutes, depending on their type and purpose. Some patients, such as those with chronic and multiple somatic symptoms, require a very long initial interview in order to develop rapport and initiate treatment. The other activities required of liaison psychiatric staff, such as supervision meetings and case discussions, are each likely to need 30–60 minutes.

7.10 By estimating the time required it is possible to calculate the numbers of staff required for a given workload. Experience suggests that in a four-hour session it is difficult to see more than three patients and to carry out the associated administrative work. Additional time must also be allowed for the liaison team to support other staff in the hospital. A general hospital serving 400,000 population is likely to receive up to 800 patients each year following deliberate self-harm; approximately 500 of these might be seen by the liaison team. Apart from deliberate self-harm patients, the team might expect to receive a further 150–200 referrals per annum from the A&E department and approximately 300 referrals from the medical and surgical wards.[146]

Type of staff

7.11 An adequate liaison service requires the involvement of at least one consultant psychiatrist whose main (ie not less than five weekly sessions) clinical commitment is to this work. This may involve a consultant who is half-time in general/community psychiatry and half-time in liaison psychiatry. A large hospital with several specialised units requires a full-time consultant liaison psychiatrist.

7.12   It is customary to include sub-consultant grade psychiatrists in liaison work. If they are trainees, then adequate supervision is mandatory and should be timetabled.

7.13   Much liaison psychiatric work can be performed by professionals who are not psychiatrists but work closely with psychiatrists in multiprofessional liaison teams. Clinical and health psychologists and specialist nurses may bring particular skills to liaison work as well as increase staff numbers. Much liaison psychiatric treatment is psychotherapeutic in nature, and the effectiveness of the liaison psychiatric team can be greatly enhanced by psychotherapists, lay or medical, with relevant and specifiable skills; of proven value are skills in cognitive-behavioural, brief psychoanalytic and group methods of psychological treatment. Such therapeutic skills may be brought to the team by medical, psychological, or nursing members as well as by independent professional 'psychotherapists'.

7.14   Social workers may also have skills of great importance to patients in contact with liaison psychiatric services. Whenever possible, it is important to involve them with hospital liaison psychiatric teams.

Organisation

7.15   *Responsibility*: Any team, and particularly any multiprofessional team, requires organisation, management and one person who takes clear responsibility for the team. Working relations with medical and surgical teams are usually best if a senior medical member is the spokesperson for the liaison team. This may entail the psychiatrist taking responsibility for the team or the team may evolve a different method of organising itself.

7.16   *Administration*: A liaison team administrator is essential to co-ordinate the team's activities, be the single contact point and telephone number for referrals, ensure that the record system works, and see that the technology used by the team (pagers, personal computers) is always in working order.

7.17   *Record keeping*: Every liaison team must implement an adequate system of keeping records and providing descriptive statistics of the work. Audit of the service is mandatory; without this it is not possible to evaluate the team's work. Information about proven systems can be obtained from the Royal College of Psychiatrists Liaison Group.

Management arrangements

7.18   In the past, liaison psychiatric services have usually been provided from within mental health services associated with general hospitals or by academic departments in medical schools. Recent changes in Health Service management arrangements, and the tendency for general mental health services to be more community-based and less in the general hospital, are making it necessary to rethink the management of liaison services.

7.19 Management of liaison psychiatric services has become complicated by the development in many areas of acute services NHS Trusts without mental health services which are now being organised in separate 'community' or 'mental health' trusts. The main responsibility of separate mental health trusts is tending towards general community-based mental health services, while the main responsibility of separate acute trusts is, understandably, general acute service provision. The result of these arrangements is a tendency to exclude liaison psychiatric services altogether from planning, funding and provision.

7.20 A number of different management arrangements for liaison psychiatry within hospital trusts are arising. In general, liaison services will be managed with the rest of psychiatry: this may be in a community trust or within an acute general hospital trust. There have also been instances where liaison psychiatry has become a separate directorate within an acute general hospital trust.

7.21 It is very important for liaison psychiatrists to sustain relationships with other psychiatrists, their professional peer group, to avoid professional isolation and to provide training facilities. In addition, a significant proportion of the mentally ill individuals dealt with by the liaison team will need to be referred to the appropriate general psychiatric services. Therefore, a liaison team must be professionally associated with a mental health unit, even if it is managerially associated with an acute unit.

7.22 The funding of liaison psychiatric services will be a matter for local arrangement. Traditionally, the psychiatric service to A&E and for emergencies has been provided from 'mental illness' sources of finance, but much specialist liaison work with individual firms and departments has evolved from the work of those *medical* specialties and will have to be funded from their budgets.

The role of purchasers

7.23 The purchasers of health care within the NHS are responsible for meeting the health needs of populations, for assessing the rival claims of different service-provision options, and for negotiating contracts with providers to meet predefined targets. The *Health of the Nation* key area handbook for mental illness indicates that purchasers should define responsibility in contracts with provider units for liaison psychiatry and for patients with both physical and mental illness.

7.24 Purchasers will wish to buy services for patients who attend general hospitals and who may be expected to become the patients of psychiatrists in the general psychiatric service. Most come to the hospital after self-poisoning or other self-injury, or present with behavioural manifestations of psychiatric disorder. These emergency services may be purchased as part of a general psychiatric contract, but care must be taken to ensure that adequate personnel and facilities are made available for this work. It is no longer appropriate for catchment psychiatrists to be asked vaguely to 'cover' the general hospital in addition to other, mainly community based, duties.

7.25   In addition, purchasers of acute services should expect providers effectively to meet the psychosocial needs of their patients; otherwise major health needs of the population will not be met. As there is significant psychosocial morbidity among the patients of every general hospital department, purchasers could require all providers to make proper arrangements to detect, assess and treat psychiatric disorder in patients of all acute departments.

7.26   Services should be judged in relation to four principles:

   a   They should be provided by a stated number of people whose time allocation and duties should be specified.

   b   The skills of these individuals, and their relevance to the service aims, should be stipulated.

   c   The work should be evaluated and subjected to continuing audit.

   d   The costs of the service should be calculated.

We recommend that acute services which include liaison psychiatric services that meet these criteria should be purchased. We further recommend that acute services which deny that the psychosocial needs in the general hospital have to be met, or fail to make adequate provision for them, should not be purchased.

7.27   It will usually be appropriate for the liaison psychiatric service to be funded as part of the costs of each medical directorate service. It may be convenient to provide staff who are managed professionally within mental health directorates by service agreements. Funds should not be allocated to liaison work at the expense of general mental health services.

Audit measures

7.28   Purchasers who contract with hospitals could make the availability of a liaison psychiatric service a contractual requirement and could also stipulate that such a service should develop and use clear audit measures as well as provide data on the number of patients referred to the liaison psychiatry team each year.

7.29   Provider units should regularly audit the liaison service and its impact on general care. The nature of such audits will depend on the particular service and the local circumstances but should attempt to assess the quality of care generally provided in the hospital as well as that provided by the liaison psychiatry service.

Chapter 7
Summary and recommendations

The current changes in NHS purchasing arrangements threaten the liaison psychiatry services which might fall outside the main remit of both mental health and acute medical services (para 7.19). The *Health of the Nation* key area handbook for mental illness suggests that each purchaser should have a specific contract with its provider units for liaison services (para 7.23). Each provider unit should:

1   Ensure that a consultant-led liaison psychiatry team is established, which is likely to require the number and type of staff outlined in paragraphs 7.9–7.14 above.

2   Ensure adequate record keeping of this work, which usually will entail secretarial help solely for this purpose (para 7.17).

3   Provide facilities, both on medical wards and in the accident and emergency department, that are sufficiently private, safe and properly furnished for interviews with patients concerning psychological, sexual problems and assessment of suicide risk. Such rooms are also required for members of the liaison team.

4   Regularly audit the liaison psychiatric service as a whole, the quality of psychosocial care in medical units and the deliberate self-harm service in particular (para 7.29).

Further Reading

BENJAMIN S, HOUSE A, JENKINS P. *Liaison psychiatry: defining needs and planning services.* London: Gaskell Press, 1994.

DEPARTMENT OF HEALTH. *Health of the Nation key area handbook for mental illness*, 1993: 72, 83.

Chapter 8
Training

Introduction

8.1　An improved service for patients in general medical units who have psychological or psychiatric problems requires better training of physicians, nurses, psychiatrists, psychologists and other staff.

8.2　Previous chapters of this report have indicated the importance of general medical staff having the necessary skills to detect psychological problems, manage most of them themselves, sometimes with the assistance of specialised nursing staff, and refer appropriate patients to psychiatrists or psychologists. Psychiatrists and psychologists must have the skills to assess and manage psychological disorders within the general medical setting. Present training schemes of physicians and psychiatrists are deficient in these respects, so many consultant staff will not have received such training.

8.3　It is not feasible or desirable to add to the already overburdened training schedules of junior doctors and nurses but the skills in working with psychological disorders in the general hospital are core skills and should be seen as part of basic training. In the case of physicians, the training must be integrated into current training programmes and/or be provided in special courses, for example in consultation skills, which the trainees must be encouraged to attend. In the case of psychiatrists a period of further specific training in general hospitals is required. One limitation is the fact that many established consultant psychiatrists do not possess the skills to be taught or, if they have them, their lack of formal training leaves them poorly equipped to teach these skills in a coherent way to junior staff.

Recommendations for improved training of physicians

8.4　The current training of physicians pays little or no specific attention to the psychological aspects of patient care. Such training is being introduced to the teaching of medical students and should be continued during the years as a junior doctor within the period of general professional training. Opportunities should be provided for consultants to receive this training under continuing medical education.

8.5　The *general professional training* period of physicians should include the following:

1　A specific period of interview skills (consultation) training. This is now becoming a recognised area of training (and is the subject of a forthcoming Royal College of Physicians working party report) which should be made available to all trainee physicians. Within the context of the present report, there are both general and specific aspects of interview skills that are relevant to the psychological care of medical patients. General skills include establishing rapport with the patient, allowing patients to describe their symptoms in their own words and taking a brief psychosocial and drinking history. Specific skills include detecting verbal and non-verbal cues, which indicate mood disturbance, establishing the patient's views about the cause of his/her symptoms, detecting abnormal illness behaviour and making the link between physical symptoms and emotional disorder. Adequate training of physicians in these skills will lead them to insist on a quiet, private interview room — a specific recommendation of this report.

2   The management of patients with medically unexplained symptoms, including feeding back to the patient the results of negative investigations and explaining how symptoms may develop in the absence of organic disease. The physician will do this by providing a coherent and simple explanation of how stressful life situations and psychiatric disorders can alter physiological mechanisms, symptom perception and increase anxieties about organic disease.

3   Prescription of antidepressants and other psychotropic drugs, awareness of their interaction with other medication, and a knowledge of their use in somatisation, chronic pain, delirium and the depressed physically ill patient.

4   Making the referral to a psychiatrist or psychologist. The skills of negotiating this with the patient need to be acquired.

5   Appreciation of the value that each member of the multidisciplinary team contributes to the psychological health of the patient, for example the role of the nurse, social worker, psychologist and psychiatrist.

How these recommendations can be achieved

8.6   Physicians in training need to acquire the skills to recognise and manage psychological illness as well as to judge the need for referral to the psychiatrist and his/her team. There are several ways in which these skills may be acquired:

a   *By block secondment to a department of psychiatry for a few weeks.* This, of course, has service implications but in some centres senior registrars in geriatric medicine already have a reciprocal arrangement with senior registrars in old age psychiatry to the benefit of both parties.

b   *Sessional secondment.* This is already used in some centres for senior registrar training in accident and emergency medicine.

c   *Joint ward rounds/case conferences with physician and psychiatrist.* This offers a unique opportunity for doctors in the two specialties to discuss clinical problems and provides an excellent opportunity for training. A psychosocial ward round that includes medical, psychiatric, nursing and social work staff is invaluable in this respect.

d   *Psychological treatment by the trainee physician under the supervision of the psychiatrist.* This may be an extremely productive learning experience. For example, the psychiatrist would supervise closely a physician in training who might be conducting a series of interviews with a dying patient or with one who has chronic somatisation or an alcohol problem.

  e *Formal postgraduate education.* The protected time for this activity should include junior physicians in interdisciplinary teaching concerned with the psychological care of medical patients.

8.7　Attention to one or more of these methods of training physicians is currently greater in some specialties, eg geriatric medicine and paediatrics; other specialties should now establish similar training opportunities at the higher training level.

Training of nurses

8.8　The basic training under Project 2000 includes some experience in mental health nursing, but many RGN trained nurses lack confidence or skills; this inhibits them from asking questions about psychological problems. Further specific training is required to develop these skills (see paras 3.5, 3.10) but such training will be ineffective unless accompanied by ongoing support from a liaison nurse. Only if such support is readily available will nurses be prepared to ask patients in general medical units about depression, suicidal ideas and alcohol/relationship problems.

8.9　Since many ward-based nurses have not received such training in the past, one set of training programmes must be aimed at qualified nurses with several years of general medical nursing experience (including, for example, specialist diabetic, cancer and renal nurses). A second set of training programmes will be required for student nurses or those recently qualified who have had some previous training in this area. Yet further courses are required to enable nursing staff to develop specialised advanced communication skills and counselling and behavioural therapeutic techniques applicable to general medical units. A national curriculum for professional training in psychiatric liaison nursing is needed.

Recommendations for improved training of psychiatrists

8.10　The case has been made for each provider unit to have a consultant psychiatrist with responsibility for liaison psychiatry. This mandates a rapid expansion in the number of consultants specialising in this work. Some will be full-time liaison psychiatry posts; many more will be special interest posts with a minimum of five sessions for liaison work. Such expansion cannot be achieved within a short timescale because of the lack of training opportunities:

  a Currently only a few centres offer a thorough training by experienced liaison psychiatric consultant trainers.

  b Some training schemes in liaison psychiatry offer little more than assessment of patients in the general wards following deliberate self-harm, thus denying the trainee liaison psychiatrist the opportunity to work in close collaboration with physicians in the assessment and management of other clinical problems and of involvement in liaison meetings with other staff. It is essential that the training posts provide the future consultant with a broad view of what the liaison psychiatrist has to offer in the general hospital.

c   The content of liaison psychiatry training has not previously been clearly defined. This can now be done in terms of the patient groups listed in Chapter 2.

8.11   Liaison psychiatrists should acquire the following skills:

a   Be fully conversant with the ways of achieving a full assessment of a patient presenting with somatisation;[147] this may be successful only if the patient's resistance to referral is overcome by using a flexible approach and by working closely with the referring physician.

b   Be able to assess mood in a physically ill patient, with a view to deciding on appropriate management. The psychiatrists should be familiar with the treatments for depression in the physically ill, including antidepressants, ECT, cognitive therapy, supportive therapy, and working with medical and nursing staff to change their interaction with the patient (eg to allow ventilation and support or alter their response to requests for analgesia). The psychiatrist must be able to participate in a shared management plan for coexisting physical and psychological disorders, such as occurs with stroke and depressive disorder or diabetes and eating disorder.

c   Be able to manage problematic illness behaviour, in the presence or absence of physical illness.

d   Be able to assess, and work out a management plan with physician colleagues, for patients with factitious disorders.

e   Work closely with other psychiatric colleagues to ensure that patients seen in the general medical units who misuse alcohol or drugs and/or are seen after an episode of deliberate self-harm receive satisfactory immediate and continuing care.

f   Be able to teach and supervise junior medical staff, nurses and others how to assess patients following deliberate self-harm, with special reference to assessment of mood and suicidal risk. Be able to teach and supervise the assessment of alcohol and substance misuse, including supervision of a withdrawal regime.

g   Be able to contribute to discussions at physicians' meetings (eg grand rounds) in such a way that the management of psychological problems of patients in medical units becomes respected as an important aspect of patient care.

h   Be able to encourage and support nursing and medical staff to hold private interviews with patients who are dying or who have sexual or relationship problems.

i   Be able to partake in collaborative research and audit projects concerning psychological care of patients in a medical unit.

8.12 *Format of training:* Some of the skills set out in paragraph 8.11 should be acquired by all psychiatrists as part of general professional training at SHO and registrar level. Further specialty experience for trainees in liaison psychiatry should be obtained at senior registrar level on a liaison psychiatry unit. The content and length of such higher training, which should be based on the skills listed above, should be specified by the Joint Committee on Higher Psychiatric Training.

Chapter 8
Summary and recommendations

In order to bring about the improvements in psychological care of medical patients reviewed in this report, improved training of staff is needed. It is recommended that:

1   The training of liaison psychiatrists, physicians and nurses must be improved along the lines set out in paragraphs 8.6, 8.9 and 8.11.

2   Training committees in each College should establish ways in which these aspects of training can be incorporated into existing training programmes.

3   The liaison psychiatrist and other members of the team should be involved in training physicians, nursing and other general hospital staff.

4   Questions relevant to the psychological aspects of patient care should regularly occur in undergraduate and relevant postgraduate examinations, including assessment of clinical skills.

5   Programmes of continuing professional development should seek ways in which physicians, psychiatrists, nurses, psychologists and social workers can meet to exchange skills and receive joint training.

Further Reading

HOUSE A, CREED F. Training in liaison psychiatry. *Psychiatric Bulletin* 1993; **17**: 95–6.

GOLDBERG D, GASK L, O'DOWD T. The treatment of somatization: teaching techniques of reattribution. *Journal of Psychosomatic Research* 1989; **32**: 137–44.

GOLDBERG D. The management of medical outpatients with non-organic disorders: the reattribution model. In: Creed F, Mayou R, Hopkins A, eds. *Medical symptoms not explained by organic disease.* Royal College of Psychiatrists and Royal College of Physicians of London, 1992: 53–9.

MAGUIRE P, FAULKNER A. How to improve the counselling skills of doctors and nurses in cancer care. *British Medical Journal* 1988; **297**: 847–9.

APPENDIX A
Psychiatric disorders frequently encountered in the general hospital: definitions and symptoms

Concept of psychiatric disorder

A.1   Standardised criteria for making a psychiatric diagnosis have evolved over a number of years and are published in the *International Classification of Diseases* (ICD-10) *Classification of Mental and Behavioural Disorders* (WHO, 1992) and in the *American Diagnostic and Statistical Manual of Mental Disorders* (DSM-IV).[10] These diagnostic guidelines rely on the number and severity of clinical symptoms to make the diagnosis. The following example, referring to depression in the general hospital setting, will illustrate this point.

A.2   Patients often become miserable and upset in response to physical illness and hospitalisation. Most cope with this well, but there is a gradation of severity of symptoms from the normal reaction to one where marked symptoms of distress fulfil the criteria for psychiatric disorder.

A.3   At the *first level*, upset and worry may be regarded as the normal and understandable emotional reactions to pain, disability, life-threatening illness and side effects of treatment. At the *second level* the emotional reaction may be more severe, but has not yet reached the level where it is clearly one of psychiatric disorder, and does not require specific treatment other than a sympathetic ear. At the *third level* the disturbance is clearly abnormal, constituting one of the disorders defined below. There are no hard and fast boundaries between these levels, ie between what is normal distress, borderline symptom and pathological disorder. Of the disorders described below, adjustment disorder is the mildest and depressive disorder the most severe.

Adjustment disorder

A.4   An adjustment disorder is a marked reaction to an identifiable stress which leads to a change in mood or behaviour that in turn leads to impairment of social or occupational functioning. The manifestations include:

■   depressed mood, anxiety, worry;

■   a feeling of inability to cope, plan ahead, continue in the same situation;

■   liability to dramatic behaviour or outbursts of emotion or violence;

■   development of bodily symptoms.

None of these symptoms is marked enough to merit a diagnosis of depressive disorder (see below).

A.5   The difference between adjustment disorder and depression is that adjustment disorder does not reach the severity and pervasiveness which would enable it to meet the full specified criteria for depression.

A.6 Certain personalities and those who lack social support are especially prone to develop adjustment disorder while in hospital. Those with particularly severe physical illness are also likely to do so. Adjustment disorder may therefore be anticipated in patients in the coronary care unit, or in chronic, disabling disorders, such as diabetes, multiple sclerosis or cancer, both at the time of initial diagnosis and when coping with relapses.

Anxiety disorder

A.7 For a diagnosis of anxiety disorder to be made, the patient must have experienced the following symptoms over several days:

Apprehension — worries about future misfortunes, feeling 'on edge', difficulty in concentrating.

Motor tension — restless fidgeting, tension headaches, trembling, inability to relax.

Autonomic over-activity — lightheadedness, sweating, fast pulse or rapid breathing, abdominal discomfort, dizziness, dry mouth.

And/or suffered several panic attacks.

A.8 A *panic attack* is a discrete period of apprehension or fear, accompanied by at least four of the following symptoms:

- breathlessness
- palpitations
- chest pain or discomfort
- choking or smothering sensation
- dizziness or unsteady feelings
- feelings of unreality
- tingling of hands or feet
- hot and cold flushes
- sweating
- faintness
- trembling or shaking

If the patient experiences these physical symptoms of anxiety during well defined attacks (usually precipitated by a particular situation, for example leaving the house) the condition is known as 'panic disorder'.

Depressive disorder

Typical

A.9 The diagnosis of depressive disorder requires: consistently depressed mood *or* loss of interest and pleasure for a minimum of two weeks, accompanied by four or more of the following symptoms:

- feelings of worthlessness or guilt
- loss of energy and fatigue
- altered appetite and weight
- retardation or agitation
- impaired concentration
- thoughts of suicide
- changed sleeping pattern

Depression may be graded as mild, moderate or severe according to the number of symptoms and the degree of disability they cause (WHO ICD-10).

Masked

A.10   Although many people have typical depression, some patients have 'masked depression' where the disorder of mood is minimal or denied. Other symptoms such as weight loss, insomnia and pain are present. There may have been a previous history of depressive disorder and predisposing or precipitating factors. This clinical picture usually responds to treatment with antidepressants.

Cause and diagnosis of psychiatric disorders in the physically ill

A.11   Diagnosis is sometimes complicated because of an overlap between the symptoms of depression (eg reduced energy, diminished appetite) and physical disorder. The clinician must decide whether there are sufficient symptoms of depressive disorder independent of the underlying physical one. This may be aided by the use of a *Beck Depression Inventory* (see Appendix C).

A.12   For half to two-thirds of patients developing anxiety and depressive disorders in the general hospital, the psychiatric disorder is a reaction to the physical illness.[148,149] This means that these disorders are more common in the most severe illnesses. Other people develop anxiety/depression in the general hospital not because of severe illness but because of their vulnerability to stress owing to a constitutional liability or lack of social support. As well as being disturbing in themselves, psychiatric disorders may be associated with poor compliance. For example, patients with pre-existing psychiatric disorder are less likely to comply with the doctor's recommendation of reduced smoking following a heart attack.[150]

Organic psychiatric disorders

Delirium

A.13   This syndrome is characterised by disturbances of consciousness and attention, perception, thinking, memory, psychomotor behaviour, emotion and the sleep-wake cycle. It may occur at any age but is most common after the age of 60 years. The delirious state is transient and of fluctuating intensity. It is due to metabolic disturbance affecting the brain, including alcohol withdrawal and prescribed drugs.

Dementia

A.14   Dementia is a syndrome caused by disease of the brain, usually of a chronic or progressive nature, in which there are disturbances of multiple higher cortical functions, including memory, thinking, orientation, comprehension, calculation, learning capacity, language and judgement. Consciousness is not clouded. Impairments of cognitive function are commonly accompanied by disturbances of emotion and social behaviour.

APPENDIX B
Unexplained physical symptoms in the medical clinic: their cause and diagnosis

B.1 Patients with bodily symptoms may attend the doctor for several reasons other than clear organic disease.[25] The symptoms may be explained by:

- Recent social stress. People who have recently been bereaved, for example, are known to consult the doctor with a variety of bodily symptoms including fatigue, headaches, palpitations and chest pains.[151]

- Symptoms may be taken to the doctor because the patient is very worried about having serious organic disease. This also often occurs in the context of recent bereavement, where the fear may be of the same disease that led to the death, or other stress, including marked family or marital conflicts.

- Some symptoms may have a pathophysiological basis, such as hyperventilation, autonomic arousal, muscular tension, aerophagy, which are normal physiological responses to stress.[152,153]

Fears of illness

B.2 Most patients with medically unexplained symptoms are adequately managed by the GP; those referred to medical outpatients are usually very concerned about the possibility of organic disease. For example, 60% of headache patients presenting to the neurologist were concerned that a brain tumour or impending stroke was the cause of the headache.[26]

Psychiatric disorder

B.3 In some patients the physical symptoms are found to be the presenting feature of an underlying psychiatric disorder; examples include palpitations due to anxiety, or weight change caused by depression. Of patients with atypical chest pain, 40–70% have anxiety.[22] Approximately 45% of patients presenting with fatigue or abdominal pain have psychiatric disorder, with depression being the most common diagnosis.[28,29] Patients with irritable bowel syndrome who develop depression also have worsened bowel symptoms.[27]

Somatisation

B.4 Most patients who present to the GP with psychiatric disorders do so with bodily (somatic) symptoms.[154] There may be no signs of overt distress, patients may not volunteer psychological symptoms nor do they consider themselves psychiatrically unwell, making diagnosis of the underlying psychiatric disorder difficult. Such patients do not recognise the connection between the bodily symptoms and the concurrent psychosocial problems; the doctor may need to help the patient make this link.[96,147]

B.5 A number of reasons have been suggested to explain why some patients 'somatise' their depression.[155] For example, the patient may pay selective attention to the bodily symptom to the exclusion of the psychological symptoms. Alternatively, patients may not wish to disclose their psychological problems, preferring to mention only the bodily symptoms for the doctor to evaluate; doctors can unwittingly reinforce this view if they respond with greater interest to physical symptoms than to psychological symptoms. Such 'differential reinforcement' by the doctor may be echoed by the family, where relatives pay more attention to physical symptoms than to psychological problems. Whereas seeking help from the doctor for physical illness is free of negative connotations, the social stigma attached to psychiatric disorders remains and may underlie the reluctance of some patients to accept, or even discuss, possible psychological reasons for their symptoms.

Some groups are especially likely to present psychological problems in the form of bodily symptoms. Special care is required in the assessment of symptoms in the following: elderly people, people from ethnic minorities and people with learning difficulties.

Keeping an open mind

B.6 Not all bodily symptoms can be explained even after organic and psychological causes have been sought. It must be remembered that not all medically unexplained symptoms are psychogenic and it is preferable to regard them as 'undiagnosed' until further investigations reveal whether organic or psychological problems, or both, are responsible. Even when a psychological problem is found it must be linked to the presenting symptoms. This area of medicine therefore demands a high degree of diagnostic acumen. Sometimes patients must be kept under periodic observation until the reason for the symptoms is clear; in one series of new outpatients a quarter were observed in this way.[156] Doctors should resist the temptation to continue investigating for organic disease unless they consider a positive diagnosis is a serious possibility.

Chronic multiple unexplained symptoms

Chronic somatisation, somatoform and conversion disorders

B.7 The second row of data in Table 2.3 (page 13) indicates that up to a fifth of patients who do not have an organic diagnosis are diagnosed as having somatisation disorder/hypochondriasis. These are patients who have chronic symptoms in numerous bodily systems that are distressing and disabling but which cannot be explained on the basis of organic disease. Such patients have been referred to as 'thick file patients', 'heart sink' patients, the 'chronic complainer' and the 'albatross syndrome'. Although they form a relatively small group, they use a disproportionate amount of health service resources.

B.8 The main features of somatisation disorder are multiple, recurrent and frequently changing physical symptoms, which have usually been present for several years and are reflected in a long and complicated history of contact with both primary and specialist medical services, during which many negative investigations or even fruitless operations may have been carried out. Symptoms may be referred to any part or system of the body, but gastrointestinal conditions (pain, belching, regurgitation, vomiting, nausea etc) and abnormal skin conditions (itching, burning, tingling, numbness, soreness and blotchiness) are among the commonest. Sexual and menstrual complaints are also common. The disorder is often associated with long-standing disruption of social, interpersonal and family behaviour. The disorder is far more common in women than in men and usually starts in early adult life.

B.9   A characteristic feature of this group of disorders is repeated and persistent requests for medical investigations, in spite of previous negative findings and reassurance by doctors that the symptoms have no physical basis. If any physical disorders are present, they do not explain the nature and extent of the symptoms or the distress and preoccupation of the patient. Even when the onset and continuation of the symptoms bear a close relationship to unpleasant life events or to difficulties or conflicts, the patient usually resists attempts to discuss the possibility of psychological causation; this may even be the case in the presence of obvious depressive and anxiety symptoms. The degree of understanding, either physical or psychological, that can be achieved about the cause of the symptoms is often disappointing and frustrating for both patient and doctor.

Problematic illness behaviour

B.10   Chronic somatising disorders have in common 'abnormal illness behaviour'. This term describes behaviours that reflect an individual's excessive concern about underlying physical disease, and the consequent search for medical treatment, which are quite out of proportion to the realistic chance of the bodily symptom representing underlying physical disease. The behaviours form a syndrome which may be observed in patients in any medical and/or surgical specialty. Its features are:[157]

- Disability disproportionate to detectable disease

- A relentless search for causes and cures

- Adoption of lifestyle around the sick role, with a repertoire of behaviours to sustain the sick role

- Reinforcement of sick role by family, disability payments, and health care providers.

B.11   There are a number of factors which lead to such behaviours. The patient may have marked personality problems, sometimes arising from adverse childhood experiences, and there also may be current relationship difficulties which may initially be denied by the patient. The person may have experienced organic disease during childhood, either themselves or in their parents, and there may also be current organic or depressive illnesses in addition to the somatising syndrome.

Factitious disorder

B.12   A few patients present to the doctor with various physical symptoms and signs that are eventually found to be self-induced. Examples are self-induced skin lesions such as dermatitis artefacta, or abnormal laboratory results, such as hyperthyroidism from ingesting thyroxin and hypoglycaemia from taking oral anti-diabetic tablets or injections. Surreptitious laxative abuse and factitious pyrexia are also recognised. In Munchausen syndrome simulated disease presents dramatically to A&E departments. Patients with factitious disorders who may have been neglected or unwanted as children appear to gain reward by entering and maintaining the sick role.[39]

B.13   Patients with factitious disorder are usually aware of the deception involved in their claimed illness even though the disorder appears to confer no obvious advantage to them. They appear to be driven by underlying psychopathology which drives them to sustain their contrivance often at considerable risk to their health. It often transpires that the patient has previous experience of organic disease (either in themselves or through working in the medical/nursing sphere) and a personality disorder with pronounced dependent, masochistic and hostile traits.

Understanding the disorders

B.14   The chronic somatising disorders are difficult for many doctors to understand because the traditional 'medical model' has little to offer by way of explanation. Instead, it is a set of behaviours that leads to diagnosis. There are different approaches to understanding these disorders: *clinicians* have written in terms of psychiatric diagnosis (see above), *physiologists* in terms of pain mechanisms, *psychologists* have examined the role of symptom development and the seeking of medical care in terms of a learning model, and *sociologists* have studied the influences of beliefs, values and roles upon the manifestations of disease and behaviour of sick people ('illness behaviour' and 'sick role').[25] These approaches will briefly be reviewed here; the reader will notice there is some overlap between the different models.

B.15   *Pain mechanisms:* A wealth of psychological influences have been shown to be important in the experience and expression of pain, including mood and personality variables, attention and other perceptual processes, expectations, and reinforcer contingencies. In addition, the experience of pain itself may provoke a variety of psychological and psychiatric reactions, including depression and anxiety, sleep problems, social withdrawal, and physical and emotional dependence on others, all of which can exacerbate pain. For example, depression and sleep loss lower the pain threshold, and a patient who depends on another person for support and help becomes very anxious if that support is threatened, so exacerbating the pain and reinforcing the dependence. An understanding of the possible significance of such processes is important in the comprehensive assessment of the patient who is in pain (see also Appendix E).

B.16   *Psychological mechanisms:* 1. The patient experiences physiological arousal, which leads to bodily sensations, such as palpitations, bowel movements, lightheadedness etc, which may be misinterpreted as indicating physical disease. 2. The patient pays selective attention to these bodily symptoms. 3. The patient uses avoidance behaviours. Thus a patient with irritable bowel syndrome may misinterpret the diarrhoea as indicating organic disease, may selectively attend to it (ie ignore periods of normal bowel habit) and may avoid leaving the house because of fear of diarrhoea; a phobic response may develop and the mere prospect of leaving the house causes anxiety and associated diarrhoea. Another patient may misinterpret palpitations as indicative of an impending heart attack and respond by lying down thus reducing the palpitations. This may lead to avoidance behaviour whereby the slightest suggestion of a quickening heart beat leads the patient to lie down and avoid going out and leading a normal life.[114]

B.17   *Illness behaviour:* This refers not to the origin of the symptom(s) and bodily sensations but to the person's response to them.[158] At times these may be ignored, at others they are taken to the doctor. Mechanic has illustrated the process using medical students; their partial knowledge about serious diseases may lead them wrongly to attribute normal physical sensations to serious diseases instead of to exhaustion, indigestion and stress as they might have done previously.[158] Other factors which determine a person's response to symptoms include the individual's personality, emotional state, and recent and past experience of illness. Those who, when children, experienced illness themselves or in their parents may be at particular risk of interpreting bodily sensations as indicators of severe disease. Recent stress, such as bereavement or social isolation, may also lead to medical consultation for trivial symptoms.

B.18   *The 'sick role':* This refers to the relief experienced, by an ill person, from the normal obligations of daily life such as going to work, supporting others, self-care etc. Such relief is generally appropriate and short-lived for acute illness. For relapsing or chronic illness, however, the prolonged relief from normal obligations may allow the individual to be excused from an unhappy work situation or from family/marital conflicts and lead to prolongation of the sick role. Other family members may unwittingly collude with this. The doctor may also contribute by allowing prolonged sick leave and/or by performing investigations which signify to the patient, the family and the employers that it is appropriate for the person to continue in the sick role. The prospect of financial compensation may also be a factor contributing to this prolongation.

A guide to recognition and management of psychological disorders associated with medically unexplained symptoms

Recognition of initial clues

C.1 The physician may be alerted to the presence of medically unexplained symptoms by a number of clues:

- the patient may have a fat folder representing numerous medically unexplained symptoms which have led to many referrals in different departments of the hospital;

- the symptoms themselves may not be typical of organic disease; they may be numerous, affecting many systems, and vary over time;

- the patient's disability may be out of proportion to an underlying organic disease, if present;

- the patient may cry during the interview, show excessive pessimism about the prognosis or demonstrate exaggerated disability, including undue sensitivity on examination;

- the patient may be accompanied by a relative who intrudes into the conversation and tends to 'reinforce' the patient's account of the symptoms and disability.

Recognition of psychological disorders and social problems

C.2 A brief clinical interview is required to confirm or refute the presence of definite anxiety, depression or adjustment disorder.[98] The interview should also elicit key psychological and social problems and should include an assessment of the patient's attitude towards his or her illness. Some patients may deny mood disturbance or feel threatened by direct questions about mood and the suggestion that the problem is a psychological one. It is therefore best initially to avoid the use of the terms 'anxiety', 'depression' and 'stress'.

C.3 The doctor should always ask:

1 *'When did you last feel quite well?'* This enables the patient to indicate the time course of the bodily symptoms, which may have commenced at the time of a stressful event. The original feeling of being unwell may have included psychological symptoms prior to the current bodily symptoms.

2 *'What do you think the symptoms are due to?'* This question enables fears of illness to be detected and explored.

C.4 Questions used to detect *adjustment disorder* are similar to those for anxiety and depression, although the symptoms are not so marked.

xx ref

The questions to confirm an *anxiety disorder* should begin with the somatic symptoms (see Appendix A, paras A.7, A.8). The bodily symptoms are usually described spontaneously; the mood symptoms may have to be asked for specifically. For patients who resist the idea that their bodily symptoms are due to anxiety, it is wise to use the techniques suggested below concerning masked depression.

C.5 The questions asked to confirm a *depressive disorder* are as follows:

Work and interests, concentration, and energy or fatigue — Ask simple questions on all these topics

Mood — eg 'Have you been feeling low, depressed or tearful?'

Ability to enjoy — eg 'Have you been able to enjoy yourself normally?'

Guilt/worthlessness — eg 'Have you tended to blame yourself or feel guilty recently?'

Future — eg 'What does the future seem like? Are there times when it seems bleak or hopeless?'

Suicidal feelings — eg 'Have you had the feeling that life is not worth living? Have there been times when you have wished you were dead, for instance that you could go to sleep but not wake up? Have you had any thoughts of harming yourself?'

Sleep, appetite, weight — Questions relating to these topics should have been asked in the routine medical history

Discovering masked depression

xx ref

C.6 In masked depression, symptoms such as fatigue, poor concentration, lack of enjoyment are present without overt disorders of mood. Such patients often resist direct questions about mood disturbance, and may even be frankly angry at the suggestion. Techniques used for such patients have been outlined in a general discussion of interviewing techniques for somatising patients (paras C.17–C.20).[147] Rather than asking patients directly if they are depressed it may be best to ask about the various symptoms which make up the diagnosis of depression, using the terms 'tiredness', 'not really fit', 'generally ill' rather than the specific term 'depression'. Patients may agree that in general they are not enjoying life, are not particularly keen on going out and are starting to get irritable. The physician may enquire if the patient relaxes easily, and how. Although patients may say they can handle stress, it is worth asking what sort of things make them keyed up. A review of all the patient's symptoms should begin with the bodily ones, including the physical symptoms of depressive disorder, and, especially if mood disturbance is denied, a link should be sought with social stresses, some of which may be difficult to detect. For example, the patient may be caught in a 'Catch 22' situation, such as having an elderly relative who is demanding of the patient yet makes him/her feel guilty if the demands are not met. Similarly, a patient may be trapped in a job where there are clear interpersonal difficulties, yet the patient feels unable to leave.

Managing the patient with somatic presentations of psychological problems

C.7   If the physician decides that organic disease is unlikely to be the cause of the symptom(s), a management plan is needed which (a) addresses the patient's worries about serious illness and coexisting life problems, (b) includes the minimum number of investigations, (c) provides an explanation for the symptoms that is acceptable to the patient and (d) offers treatment for anxiety/depression if present. The patient can be adequately managed only if his or her particular worries have been elicited in the history.[166]

Explanation and reassurance

C.8   Too often doctors, believing they are reassuring the patient, state that the symptoms are not due to organic disease. Unfortunately patients often feel they are being told there is nothing the matter and are left either believing that the physician has not understood their symptoms or wondering whether they have some sinister disease that has not been diagnosed. This means that any explanation must be given carefully in terms that the patient understands, and any reassurance based firmly on a knowledge of the patient's particular worries.

C.9   A symptom may have a specific physiological-pathophysiological mechanism,[152] eg hyperventilation can be explained and has a specific treatment, or a more general explanation may be appropriate. Another symptom for which an explanation can be given is abdominal pain which is aggravated by food and eased by bowel action. In this case a picture of the colon may be shown with an explanation that after a meal messages go to the colon to contract and that if the bowel is over-active a more violent contraction occurs which is painful and a bowel action relieves such pain. It must of course have been previously established that this explanation fits with the patient's reported symptoms.

C.10   After a physiological explanation for the pain has been given *and* understood, it is then possible to explain the psychogenic factors that are involved. In the case of abdominal pain, for example, the gut becomes over-reactive and tender and so causes pain. An analogy with increased respiration and 'butterflies' caused by anxiety prior to attending the dentist, for example, may be helpful.

A satisfactory physiological explanation for the perceived somatic symptoms does not always exist. For example, the previously postulated relationship between muscle contraction and tension headache has been shown not to hold, and the physiological cause of many headaches remains uncertain. Nevertheless it seems helpful, whenever possible, to talk to such patients in physiological terms which they can readily understand.

The role of investigations

C.11   Some investigations may be necessary because diagnostic doubt remains after a history and physical examination. They should be planned appropriately in order to clarify any differential diagnosis, and not be seen as 'fishing' with the general supposition that there might be an organic cause for the symptoms. The doctor may feel it appropriate to tell the patient, prior to the investigation, that the symptoms suggest a disorder of function, rather than organic disease. The normal results will then help increase the confidence of the patient that there is no organic cause for the symptoms, particularly if normal findings are congruent with the doctor's predictions.

C.12   Obviously what is considered appropriate investigation varies according to the clinical circumstances. Aspects to be considered include costs and risk, as well as the sensitivity and specificity, of the investigations. The possibility of litigation is also a factor which may influence a doctor's decision to perform investigations. Investigations also carry a disadvantage in so far as abnormalities may be revealed which are not the cause of the patient's illness. An example might be a hiatus hernia seen on barium swallow, which does not explain the patient's sensations of bloating and fullness after a meal (hiatus hernia is present in 30% of an asymptomatic population).

C.13   Very often a full explanation is sufficient to dispel anxieties without technical investigation. In one study of patients with headaches, 60% had substantial fears about organic disease, notably the risks of brain tumour or an impending stroke. In the great majority, reassurance was readily achieved, and the extent of the reassurance and patient satisfaction was not linked to the extent of the technical investigation of headaches. However, in another study from the USA, patients with chest pain were randomly assigned to receive investigations considered by the attending physician as clinically unnecessary (an electrocardiogram and creatine phosphokinase). Those patients who received these investigations did evaluate their care as better than did those who were not investigated. There is thus a danger that patients may be seduced by quantity of technical investigation, and, as resources for health care are limited, purchasers and clinicians together will have to determine just how much technical investigation can be undertaken for the purposes of reassurance.

C.14   Informing the patient that an investigation is negative requires skill, and should be undertaken in awareness of the patient's prior worries. It is necessary not to leave the patient thinking 'if that's not the matter, then what *is* the trouble?', still focusing upon the possibility of an organic disease.

C.15   Some patients who present with a somatised psychological problem rapidly accept the link with psychosocial difficulties once these are brought up at interview (so-called 'facultative somatisers').[154,33] Others resist the approach, in which case reattribution techniques are appropriate; direct questioning about psychosocial factors may also be met with resistance and more detailed enquiries are necessary.

Assessment questionnaires used in population surveys are listed at the end of this Appendix.

Reattribution techniques

C.16   If the patient attributes his/her symptoms to physical disease, but the doctor considers the underlying problem is probably of a psychological nature, it is not simply a matter of converting the patient to the doctor's point of view. The doctor must first be sure of the link in order to be sure that the psychological symptoms really are related to the somatic symptoms. This is achieved by careful enquiry as to the time course of the symptoms in relation to social stress and psychological disturbance. In this way the patient may come to realise that the somatic symptoms are linked to the psychological problems and may 'reattribute' the cause of the symptoms to the underlying psychological problem. If not, the doctor may use the following specific techniques to achieve this.

C.17   *Feeling understood:* The patient must feel understood. This requires that the doctor takes a full history, examines the patient and considers carefully the results of investigations that have been performed. Useful aspects of history taking that are sometimes overlooked are:

- taking a full history of the symptom, including times of the day when it is better or worse (these may link to certain situations);

- responding to verbal and non-verbal cues with clarifying and empathic comments;

- exploring family situation and attitudes;

- exploring fully the patient's ideas regarding the origin of the symptom and its significance.

If these steps are not followed the doctor runs the risk, later in the interview, of dismissing the symptoms as 'all in the mind'.

C.18   *Changing the agenda:* The doctor feeds back to the patient the pertinent (often negative) findings of examination and investigation but, in doing so, acknowledges the reality of the pain. The doctor is then in a position to change the agenda from the search for organic disease to looking at other possible causes for the pain, including tension and stress.

C.19   *Making the link:* This is the final step, when the doctor can help the patient to realise the link between the pain and the stress, anxiety or depression that has been elicited earlier in the interview.

C.20   The following techniques may also be useful in helping the doctor to explain how psychological problems lead to bodily symptoms:

- Simple explanation — eg anxiety causes symptoms, by hyperventilation or tachycardia; depression does so by lowering the pain threshold by causing loss of weight or fatigue.

- Physiological demonstration — eg holding a book on an outstretched hand indicates that tension in muscles can cause pain but this does not indicate organic disease in the muscles. Alternatively, asking the patient to hyperventilate in the clinic may induce bodily symptoms.

- Keeping a diary may demonstrate the temporal link between onset or exacerbation of pain and stress, eg onset following marital separation and exacerbation with each aspect of the divorce settlement.

- The patient may be encouraged to realise that even discussion of the stressful situation at interview may induce the symptom.

- It may be easier for the patient to accept that the link occurs in another family member before accepting the link themselves: 'its funny, doctor, my mother had pains like this after my father died'.

Common assessment questionnaires used in population surveys

C.21   *General health questionnaire*[159] measures psychological distress. This might give misleading high scores because the presence of physical illness leads to marking some somatic items (eg appetite and weight loss, poor sleep).

Hospital Anxiety and Depression Questionnaire[160] was designed to be used in the general hospital setting and excludes somatic items.

Beck Depression Inventory[168] measures severity of depression.

Whiteley Index[161] is a measure of illness concerns, sometimes known as 'hypochondriasis'. This scale forms one subscale of the Illness Behaviour Questionnaire.[162]

The Suicide Intent Scale is one of several scales that can be routinely used.[163,171]

Mini-Mental State[164] and *Newcastle Scale*[165] can be used to screen for cognitive impairment but are not diagnostic instruments. More detailed clinical interviews are required to identify the cause of low scores.

CAGE Questionnaire and *Michigan Alcoholism Screening Test (MAST)* are screening questionnaires for alcohol problems.[169]

APPENDIX D
Use of antidepressants in the medically ill

D.1   Antidepressant medication is effective in the majority of depressed patients and is usually tolerated with relatively few adverse effects. A sedative tricyclic, eg amitriptyline or dothiepin, is useful for the patient who is also anxious and sleeps poorly. Because of interactions with physical illnesses and the drugs used to treat them, dosage should be increased cautiously but full doses should be used wherever possible. The selective serotonin re-uptake blockers are more expensive but can be prescribed in patients who have cardiac disorders, glaucoma and prostatism, in whom tricyclics are contraindicated. The patient must be warned about an arousing effect that can initially exacerbate anxiety and upper gastrointestinal side effects.

D.2   There is little difference in efficacy between the different classes of antidepressants; their use is reviewed in detail by Fava.[102] Some people respond to one group; if there is no response, a drug of the other group may be tried. The selective serotonin re-uptake inhibitors may have advantages in elderly people, those with medical illness or at risk of confusion and, possibly, those with cardiac problems. Electroconvulsive therapy (ECT) is an effective treatment for severe depression that does not respond to antidepressants.

D.3   When treating patients it is important to explain the biochemical basis of the depression, that antidepressant drugs do not cause physical dependence, and that improvement will take at least two to four weeks to become apparent. It is important to emphasise the need to take the medication as prescribed and not just when the patient is feeling unwell, that the use of the drug is only the first step in helping the patient cope with the physical illness and that it may need to be taken for at least four to six months to achieve full effect and prevent relapse. If the patient does not respond to one antidepressant it is appropriate to try another from a different class.

D.4   When it comes to choosing which antidepressant to prescribe, their known side effects and potential interactions with other drugs are important in patients who are physically ill. The side effects associated with antidepressants can be grouped according to their mode of action (see Tables D.1 and D.2). With the exception perhaps of lofepramine (Gamanil) the tricyclics have more side effects and more serious side effects than the new selective serotonin re-uptake inhibitors (SSRIs) fluoxetine, fluvoxamine, sertraline and paroxetine and the selective monoamine oxidase inhibitor (MAOI) moclobemide. Overall, it tends to be the anticholinergic side effects, seen most commonly in the tricyclics, which prove the most troublesome in the physically ill and elderly. Thus, drugs such as amitriptyline and clomipramine, although undoubtedly effective as antidepressants, carry with them certain hazards. The same drugs are also highly toxic in overdose and should not be given to patients who are considered to be at risk of taking an overdose.

Table D.1
Side effects of antidepressants according to mode of action

Muscarinic	Blurred vision/precipitation of narrow-angle glaucoma, lowering of convulsant threshold, dry mouth, constipation, urinary hesitancy and retention, sinus tachycardia and heart failure, memory dysfunction, confusion
Histaminic	Weight gain, hypotension, sedation
Adrenergic	Postural hypotension, falls, tachycardia, heart failure, sexual dysfunction, tremor
Serotonergic	Nausea, weight loss, headache, occasional insomnia and agitation, loss of libido

D.5   Antidepressants are metabolised primarily by the liver. Hepatic and renal failure can compromise the metabolism and excretion of many antidepressants, leading to toxic plasma levels, although the GFR has to be markedly impaired before this becomes a clinical problem or before dose adjustments are necessary. Again the SSRIs are safer in this respect, with the exception of paroxetine which is cleared rather slowly in patients with poor renal function. Fluoxetine, owing to the long half-life of its major active metabolite, should also be used cautiously in patients with hepatic or renal disease. Sertraline is a useful and safe drug in the treatment of depression in renal failure. On the whole it is better to treat the depression in these patients than to ignore it. Plasma levels can be obtained for many of the tricyclic antidepressants and this may give them an advantage in respect of monitoring the dose. They are not a good choice of drug, however, if the patient is prone to episodes of confusion.

D.6   Although drugs with anticholinergic properties can lead to increases in heart rate, this is not usually a problem in normal clinical doses. However, in the elderly or in patients with heart disease this may precipitate heart failure. Clinically significant postural hypotension occurs in 5–20% of patients receiving tricyclic antidepressants and this can be dangerous in the elderly. Glassman *et al*[172] reported a 4% incidence of injuries from falls in patients taking imipramine. Therefore, before prescribing a tricyclic or an MAOI it is advisable to check whether there is any pre-existing postural drop and select an SSRI class of drug if hypotension looks likely to present a problem. Many tricyclics also have quinidine-like effects, thus posing a risk of heart block in patients with bundle branch disease. Trazodone can exacerbate ventricular irritability and should be used with caution too. It may therefore be advisable to lower the dose of anti-arrythmics when prescribing tricyclic antidepressants. The SSRIs and MAOIs do not cause a delay in cardiac conduction and are thus safer in this respect. The SSRIs can, however, enhance platelet aggregation which may be undesirable in patients with severe coronary artery disease. However, depression is common following myocardial infarction and the benefits from treating it in terms of eventual physical recovery and successful rehabilitation (as well as recurrence of infarction and mortality) vastly outweigh the comparatively small risks associated with the effects of these drugs on the heart.

Table D.2
Receptor affinity of antidepressant drugs indicating likely side effects

	Muscarinic	Histaminic	Adrenergic	Serotonergic
Amitriptyline	++++	++++	+++	+
Imipramine	++	++	+++	++
Clomipramine	+++	+	+++	++++
Trimipramine	++++	++++	+++	0
Desipramine	++	0	+	0
Protriptyline	++++	+	0	0
Nortriptyline	++	++	++	0
Lofepramine	+	0	+	0
Dothiepin	+	++++	++	0
Fluoxetine	0	0	0	+++
Fluvoxamine	0	0	0	+++
Sertraline	0	0	0	+++
Paroxetine	0	0	0	+++
Trazodone	0	+	+++	++
Mianserin	0	+++	+++	0
Moclobemide	0	0	++	++
Phenelzine	+	0	+++	++

D.7   The half-life of the SSRIs in the elderly is the same as in younger patients, which, with their simple fixed-dosing regime, makes them especially suitable for use in older patients.

Further Reading

BAZIRE S. *Psychotropic drug directory: the professionals' pocket handbook and aide memoire.* Lancaster: Quay Publishing Ltd, 1994.

GOLDBERG DP, BENJAMIN S, CREED F. Psychiatry in medical practice. 2nd edn. Ch7: Treatment. London, New York: Routledge, 1991.

APPENDIX E
Interdisciplinary approach to management of pain

E.1 The importance of an interdisciplinary approach to pain management is increasingly recognised by physicians and others specialising in pain management. Clinical psychologists and psychiatrists contribute to diagnosis and management, and programmes based on cognitive-behavioural principles have become the recognised standard in the rehabilitation of the chronic pain patient. A psychological perspective is relevant to all medical conditions and procedures in which pain plays a significant role, as well as to obviously psychogenic pain problems. Psychological approaches have yielded benefits in the understanding of pain mechanisms, assessment of pain, and in management.

Assessment and management of pain

E.2 *Pain nature and severity:* recognition that pain is a multidimensional phenomenon with sensory, cognitive, affective and behavioural components has had a major impact on pain assessment methods and on the management plans based on them. Simple unidimensional rating scales are inadequate; a widely used measure is the McGill Pain Questionnaire which invites the subject to endorse adjectives descriptive of pain and indicate their intensity. Scores derived from this instrument can be used 'before and after' to measure change.

E.3 *Mood:* the assessment of emotional state is important in the pain clinic as elsewhere in medical settings, and in excess of 50% of pain patients may be found on careful assessment to suffer depressive disorder. Standardised scales and inventories (eg the Beck Depression Inventory) may be useful at initial evaluation and also to monitor progress.

E.4 *Cognitions:* assessment of pain-related cognitions may be helpful. For instance, patients who consistently employ negative cognitions (eg 'catastrophising', hopelessness) report more pain than those who use more positive 'coping strategies'.

E.5 *Lifestyle:* the assessment of changes in quality of life may point to benefits from particular treatment methods. NOTE: these aspects of assessment complement, but do not supplant, detailed history taking which should include questions on family and social matters as well as on biography and history of the present illness and its treatment. Joint interviews with family members may provide invaluable information.

E.6 *Treatment of pain:* psychopharmacological treatments may be used as analgesia as well as treatment of depression and anxiety in pain patients, as in other medical populations. In addition, cognitive-behavioural programmes have been developed. These aim to produce change in (a) physiological processes presumed to underlie the pain (eg relaxation, biofeedback), (b) cognitive processes associated with the perception of pain and its impact on the patient's life (eg cognitive therapy, stress management) or (c) behavioural manifestations of pain, including 'abnormal illness behaviour' (eg operant conditioning, goal setting, activity scheduling).

APPENDIX F
Models of care for elderly people

F.1   In addition to the need to diagnose and treat recognisable syndromes, including depression, dementia and acute confusional states, there are many other aspects of psychiatric morbidity in elderly people that have influenced the development of services. A few of these are: psychiatric factors that have precipitated physical health problems and vice versa; psychiatric morbidity resulting from pharmacological treatment; the influence of psychosocial factors on the course of a medical disorder. These interact with the multiple medical diagnoses regularly discovered in many elderly people.

F.2   As has already been pointed out in a previous joint RCP/RCPsych report, *Care of elderly people with mental illness*,[20] there is marked regional variation in the availability and pattern of psychiatric services for elderly people. This was the subject of an earlier report by Wattis;[173] although the situation has improved somewhat in recent years, there is still a marked variability in the quantity and quality of the services available. In general, albeit with some notable exceptions, there has been a trend to establish separate departments of psychiatry for elderly people within the psychiatry unit, many of whom work closely with their geriatrician colleagues. Where this is the case, joint ward rounds and clinics involving senior staff from both services is probably the most frequent approach. In many other instances the interface is serviced on the basis of a consultation service. A joint approach often leads to earlier discharge of patients as each team has confidence in the support of the other, and access to their facilities and resources if appropriate, as well as the benefits of a joint management approach whilst the patient is in hospital.

F.3   Despite the advantages of an integrated approach, it must not be forgotten that some patients' problems are probably best treated within one specific clinical setting; for example, severely depressed or behaviourally disturbed demented people are probably best managed primarily within a psychiatric setting whilst those with confusional states secondary to drugs or the toxic effects of illness are often best managed within a geriatric or general medical setting. In between these two extremes there are many people who could be well looked after jointly by the geriatric and old age psychiatry team, irrespective of the setting.

F.4   The interface between geriatrics and old age psychiatry has been reviewed by Bendall.[170] At the simplest level, as already described, there are reciprocal visits by senior staff to each of the units. In others the outpatient and day hospital facilities, and some of the short stay beds, are geographically close together. This allows better cross-consultation between the medical and non-medical staff involved, with readier exchange of advice.

F.5   In Nottingham, the University Department of Health Care of the Elderly comprises physicians and psychiatrists working closely together. Collaboration involves not just the practice of medicine and psychiatry but also teaching and research involving a whole range of disciplines.

F.6   In summary, where resources allow, there is a trend towards a more integrated pattern of working between geriatricians and old age psychiatrists. The degree of integration ranges from reciprocal weekly ward visits on the one hand, to the almost complete integration of the two departments on the other. In between there are many other models of service provision, the nature of which depends upon the philosophy of the consultants involved and the practicalities of their working environments. The establishment of a joint assessment unit does not necessarily require additional resources; it can often be accomplished by the reorganisation of existing facilities.

F.7   The establishment of closer working relationships between physicians in general medicine and old age psychiatry services is clearly important, and could probably be achieved given goodwill and a willingness to adjust working practices and attitudes in those areas where an old age psychiatry service, with adequate resources, exists. The value of this has recently been reviewed. The introduction of an old age psychiatry consultation service in a general hospital setting led to a drop in the number of referrals of patients with acute confusion, or indeed with no psychiatric disorder, and an increase in the referral pattern for depression etc. This change was not observed in the same period in relation to referrals from general practice, where the case mix referred remained stable. There is therefore a suggestion that the educational influence of a consultation service is of value. The rising number of elderly people admitted to general wards is such that the degree of psychiatric morbidity already exceeds the capacity of many consultation services, and education of non-psychiatrists to detect and manage many of these disorders is going to become increasingly important.

F.8   In summary, in the United Kingdom there is a trend towards a more integrated working pattern, the pooling of resources and education of colleagues.

F.9   In the USA there has been a greater development of liaison psychiatry for elderly people. Many hospitals have a specialised geriatric/psychiatric consultation service using a team approach within the general hospital setting. In addition to medical staff this may involve a family therapist, a psychiatric nurse specialist and an old age psychiatric social worker, in varying combinations. As described above, continuing education of medical and nursing staff is considered a key role of such a service.

Health needs assessment

F.10   Patients in a general hospital have needs that may be physical, psychological or social in nature. Each of these categories requires detailed assessment beyond the scope of this Appendix; eg social assessments include the patient's social functioning and the support services required to maintain him or her in the community. These need to be considered for every patient and should constitute part of the routine assessment. To a large extent this is already the case in most departments of geriatric medicine and general medicine.

1   There are recognised assessment scales that can be employed to improve objectivity in such assessments, but many of them are too time-consuming and/or impractical in a normal day-to-day clinical setting. Nevertheless each unit needs to ensure that objective assessments of intellectual functioning, mood and social functioning are made in all old people admitted to hospital, irrespective of the setting. The College has addressed this issue elsewhere.

F.12   Elderly people with psychiatric morbidity in a general setting require access to the full range of supporting and paramedical services, eg appropriately trained nurses, occupational therapists, physiotherapists, speech therapists and social workers.

F.13   Patients require privacy when seeing their relatives and friends, and particularly to allow adequate psychiatric assessment and counselling. This is best undertaken in a room set aside for the purpose, which should be appropriately decorated and furnished. These patients will require more medical and nursing time than patients with purely physical conditions, and the staff caring for them need to be trained in the techniques that are necessary to help establish a rapport. In addition to the nursing and paramedical workers mentioned above, many will need access to a clinical psychologist.

F.14   Elderly patients with unacceptable behavioural patterns or a tendency to wander should not be unreasonably restrained; conversely, they should not be allowed to put at risk the care of others on the same ward.

F.15   Communication between all those involved in providing care may be more difficult than it is for other patients because a greater number of disciplines are likely to be involved. There may be differences of opinion on the relative priorities of management, and the terminology of one discipline may not be readily understood by another. It is therefore essential that all opinions are recorded in the patient's notes, even if a particular discipline prefers also to keep its own records.

F.16   The attitude of all staff to this type of elderly patient should be as respectful and caring as it would be to any other person in the ward, irrespective of the particular problems posed by the psychiatric aspect of their condition. Finally, all those caring for the patient should be readily available for consultation with his or her relatives.

Resources

F.17   Since there are no clear guidelines for the resources that should be provided in a liaison psychiatric service for elderly people, it would be unrealistic to suggest an appropriate level of staffing, beds, supporting services etc. Their development is likely to depend upon the local exigencies, the relationship between consultant colleagues and the present patterns of services that have evolved in each locality. We would however urge the closer integration of old age psychiatric, geriatric and general medical services in respect of the needs of the patient group described. As elsewhere within the Health Service, it is unlikely that the increasing numbers of older people will be containable within the present pattern of service delivery, even if increasing numbers of specialists in old age psychiatry and geriatric medicine were to be recruited.

F.18 The role of specialists in geriatric and psychogeriatric medicine will increasingly be that of advising colleagues and facilitating the management of their patients. This will be backed up by a core of essential services for those patients who need the specialist facilities of a geriatric and/or an old age psychiatry department. The majority of patients will have to be managed within other departments. Closer integration across service boundaries will improve education and the ability of others to detect and manage much of the psychiatric morbidity that is found in elderly patients in a general hospital setting. The time has also come to train non-medical staff, particularly nurses from the psychiatric sector, to undertake a more prominent liaison role just as they have in the community psychiatric setting, and in relation to other physical illnesses, for example the service provided to orthopaedic units in some districts by specialist nurses trained and based within the department of geriatric medicine.

F.19 More effective use of existing resources in many districts or trusts could make a significant contribution to the present situation. This would require a change of working attitudes, a pooling of facilities, and the training of nursing and/or paramedical staff to undertake what is often traditionally considered to be a medical role.

Conclusion

F.20 Many of the practices already developed, or developing, at the interface between geriatric medicine and old age psychiatry could readily be applied to the problems of elderly people with psychiatric morbidity who are patients in general medical wards. Much could be achieved in many places, but not in all without a significant increase in resources.

APPENDIX G
The psychological care of medical patients — a purchaser's guide
This guide is available as a separate publication

The issues

G.1   Psychological disorders are significantly more prevalent in medical inpatients and outpatients than in the general population. This guide is designed to enable purchasers (health authorities and general practice fundholders) to identify the nature and level of service provision that they should purchase for such patients.

G.2   Psychological problems in hospital patients, though common, are often not recognised or not adequately dealt with. Lack of privacy and time and the fact that modern medical practice is orientated toward detecting and treating organic disorder both serve to divert attention away from psychological aspects. Expensive technological investigations are carried out before psychological issues are considered. Many physicians and nursing staff have not received adequate training or developed sufficient skills to diagnose and manage complex psychological disorder to know when to refer a patient to a psychologist or psychiatrist. Patients are often reluctant to acknowledge psychological problems or accept referral.

G.3   The report seeks to address these widespread shortcomings in two principal ways: first by improvements in the training of medical and other staff in the recognition and handling of psychological problems in medical patients, and second by the development of a liaison psychiatry service in each general hospital. The recommendations on training are principally directed to the professions and to providers, though there are suggestions as to audit (para G.20). The recommendations on liaison psychiatry involve purchasers more directly.

Nature and role of a liaison psychiatry service

G.4   The term 'liaison psychiatry' describes arrangements whereby hospital physicians and surgeons have defined access to a team of psychiatrist, psychologist and other relevant health care professions for the care and treatment of patients presenting with psychiatric or psychological as well as organic symptoms. The original model of liaison psychiatry, which developed in the USA, involved the psychiatrist attending medical ward rounds and other clinical meetings. This proved expensive on time and is now used less frequently. An alternative 'consultation' model, confined to individual referrals of patients, proved much cheaper but comparatively ineffective, because referring physician and psychiatrist might not meet or see the patient together. A preferred approach, commonly known as 'liaison-consultation', has therefore emerged, involving individual consultation and regular planned meetings, and it is this approach which the Joint Report recommends.

G.5   The essence of liaison psychiatry, as described in the report, is that consultation-liaison should occur in relation to the full range of patients presenting with both organic symptoms and psychological disorder. It is not adequate, as in many hospitals at present, for the service to cover only patients admitted as a result of self-harm.

Evidence as to benefits of liaison psychiatry

Epidemiological considerations

G.6   Liaison psychiatry of its nature is concerned with situations where physical and psychological disorders overlap. The principal situations where this may occur are (a) as a psychological reaction to physical disease or (b) where a psychological disorder causes physical symptoms.

G.7   Table G.1 summarises the classification system used in the report. A glossary of terms is appended:

G.8   *Organic disease with associated psychiatric disorder.* Adjustment disorders occur in about a quarter of medical patients, while the prevalence of anxiety and depressive disorders at 12–15% is twice as high as in the general population, and can reach 25–35% in particular groups of patients. Failure to recognise and address these conditions may impair the patient's quality of life, delay recovery, increase mortality, or increase the chances of problematic illness behaviour or suicide.

G.9   *Cerebral complications of organic disease.* Delirium is detected in 10% of acute admissions while 25–35% of elderly medical inpatients have dementia. Death rates associated with delirium are higher, but patients with dementia have longer hospital stays than those without.

G.10 *Physical symptoms not due to organic disease.* Between 25% and 50% of new medical outpatients experience physical symptoms that cannot be explained on the basis of organic disease, and up to half of such patients have underlying anxiety or depression. The term 'somatisation' is used to describe this physical presentation of psychological disorder. Among this group a small proportion present with chronic multiple unexplained symptoms. It is estimated that a district with a population of 400,000 would have 17,600 presenting with some degree of somatisation while 1,200 would have chronic multiple unexplained symptoms. Both groups are expensive in terms of costs incurred for tests to eliminate organic disease and the latter are also especially expensive in terms of multiple hospital admissions (para 5.2).

G.11 *Patients who misuse alcohol/drugs.* These groups have been extensively covered in other Royal College reports and are not covered in detail in this one. The report does point out that current guidelines to detect alcohol in the general hospital are probably not being adhered to.

G.12 *Patients requiring medical assessment for treatment following deliberate self-harm.* Approximately 100,000 admissions annually occur in England and Wales, plus many patients seen in A&E departments but not admitted. The report draws attention to

Table G.1
Classification of psychiatric and psychological problems that may be encountered in general medical units

Category		Sub Category	
A	Organic disease with associated psychiatric disorder	1	Adjustment disorder
		2	Anxiety disorder
		3	Depressive disorder
B	Cerebral complications of organic disease	1	Delirium
		2	Dementia
		3	Focal defects: perceptual and personality changes
C	Physical symptoms not due to organic disease (medically unexplained symptoms)	1	Stress reactions/fears of illness and somatic presentation of psychiatric disorders: anxiety/depression (somatisation)
		2	Chronic multiple unexplained symptoms (chronic somatisation) a) Somatoform disorders b) Simulated disorders
D	Patients who misuse alcohol and drugs	1	As a cause of admission
		2	Detected during inpatient stay
E	Deliberate self-harm (DSH)	1	Inpatient following DSH
		2	Outpatient seen in A&E
F	Patients with sexual or relationship problems and eating disorders	1	Direct presentation
		2	Complicating other disease (eg diabetes)

the relevance of improved training for staff in this area to achieve *Health of the Nation* targets to reduce suicide.

G.13 *Patients with sexual or relationship problems and eating disorders.* These problems are often not detected because patients are reluctant to disclose them. Quiet interview facilities are obviously essential. Sexual problems may be straightforward to help. If an eating disorder occurs with a physical illness, such as diabetes, specialised inpatient treatment may need to be purchased.

General practice: referral to hospital

G.14 The report recognises that a significant proportion of those with a less severe degree of disorder are managed entirely by general practitioners, and the report does not seek to advise on the discharge of this role. Rather the report is concerned with the arrangements once a patient has been referred, or admitted, to hospital.

Benefits of liaison psychiatry

G.15 The main benefits which can be achieved by improved training of physicians and an effective liaison psychiatry service are earlier detection of psychological problems and hence involvement of psychiatry or psychology. In addition to the obvious health gains of reduced disability and distress with improved quality of life for patients, these changes should lead to:

1 Reduction in the number of tests seeking to find non-existent organic causes for somatisation disorders. The physician has of course responsibility for establishing that an organic cause cannot be found, but experience suggests that much repeat testing occurs at the insistence of the patient. One study showed a 40% reduction in costs of diagnostic tests as a result of a single psychiatric consultation.

2 Avoidance of inappropriate hospital admissions. The 1,200 people in a district of 400,000 who have chronic multiple unexplained disorders will have, on average, 22 abortive hospital admissions in their lifetime. This represents a major financial commitment. Assuming an admission every two years at a cost of £1,000 per admission, such patients represent abortive expenditure of £600,000 a year. The costs associated with the much larger number (17,600) with some degree of somatisation will be lower *per capita* but could well be much larger overall.

3 Reduction in length of stay. A large meta-analysis study has suggested an average reduction of 1.5 days following psychological interventions. A study specific to elderly patients with hip fractures found a reduction of 2 days.

4 Reduction in number of medical outpatient attendances of patients whose needs would be more appropriately met in other ways.

5 Identification and treatment of anxiety and depression in patients with organic, particularly serious organic, disease. The Joint Report cites studies suggesting that house physicians recognise less than half the cases of anxiety/depressive disorder or alcohol problems among their patients. Not all those recognised will receive specific help from the physician, and less than one in ten of the recognised cases are referred to an appropriate clinician. Too often physicians simply regard the condition as a natural reaction to the organic disorder rather than as one that is susceptible to treatment.

6 Reduction in subsequent medical service utilisation.

Components of a liaison psychiatry service

G.16 The Joint Report describes several models but its main proposal is for the creation of a generic liaison psychiatric team which would typically consist of a full-time consultant psychiatrist, one or more psychiatrists in training, two clinical nurse specialists, a social worker and a clinical psychologist. The very minimum consultant input to liaison psychiatry is seen as five sessions.

G.17 Alternative models are described in relation to particular specialties. Outpatient services where there are numerous patients with medically unexplained symptoms (eg neurology and gastroenterology) are seen as examples where there may be a case for joint clinics or a psychiatrist in the clinic. Cancer and diabetic care are used as examples of areas where the training of a specialist nurse already involves developing appropriate psychological assessment skills. It is recognised, however, that this approach may facilitate other clinicians in opting out. Alcohol treatment and intensive care are seen as examples where a regular liaison meeting approach is appropriate, while pain clinics and chronic fatigue are regarded as particularly suitable for a multidisciplinary assessment model.

Purchasing liaison psychiatry

G.18   The generic team is seen as the main provider of liaison psychiatry. The Joint Report specifies that services should be judged by: staffing levels and duties; skills; presence of continuing audit; and costs. Purchasers in general are reluctant to be prescriptive about staffing levels, but clearly the recommendations can be used to inform a judgement. It is also recommended that acute services should only be purchased where an adequate liaison service is included. This recommendation stems from the view that such an acute service may look cheaper in terms of the price of a completed consultant episode or an outpatient visit, but will represent less good value because a proportion of the activity will be abortive. Obviously too the Joint Report argues that a health care model which provides appropriately for psychosocial aspects should improve outcomes.

G.19   Many acute hospitals are in separate Trusts from their associated mental health services. The Joint Report argues that, whether or not the liaison psychiatry team are employees of the acute trust, the cost of the liaison psychiatry service would be included within the costs of each medical directorate service. In practice this probably means that the costs are met in the contract for acute care.

G.20   A number of audit measures are suggested. Purchasers should monitor patient referrals to liaison psychiatry as a percentage of completed episodes. Provider/professional audit would include: random sampling of case notes of patients with medically unexplained symptoms; assessment of the frequency of identification of depressive disorder; monitoring investigations yielding negative results; random patient satisfaction assessment; reduction in numbers of investigations and reduced lengths of stay. Purchasers should be able to establish that such audit processes are in place.

G.21   Introducing or extending a liaison psychiatry service, however beneficial its impact in cost/benefit terms appears in principle, carries the risk that the additional costs will be incurred without the offsetting cost savings being achieved. This is not a new experience for purchasers, but it is complicated in this instance by the fact that the savings, consisting in the first instance mainly in reductions of abortive patient episodes, will appear to involve a reduction in the activity of the provider, albeit offset by an increase in consultant referrals within episodes of care. It will be important for purchasers and providers to have a clear understanding of the probable effect on contractual volumes of introducing or extending a liaison psychiatry service.

Conclusion

G.22 The Joint Report argues that a liaison psychiatry service along the model(s) suggested is a cost-effective way of improving the treatment of medical patients with psychosocial problems, and that, provided it is introduced in a carefully controlled way, overall costs should at worst not increase while health outcomes should improve.

Glossary

G.23 (Standardised criteria for identifying a psychiatric disorder are to be found in ICD-10. The definitions below are intended only to give a broad understanding to a lay person.)

Adjustment disorder. A marked reaction to an identifiable stress, resulting in change in mood or behaviour sufficient to impair social or occupational functioning but not of the severity and pervasiveness to meet the full specified criteria for depression.

Anxiety disorder. A state in which the patient has experienced apprehension, motor tension, autonomic over-reaction and/or panic attacks over several days.

Depressive disorder (depression). Consistently depressed mood or loss of interest and pleasure for at least two weeks accompanied by four or more of: feelings of worthlessness or guilt; impaired concentration; loss of energy/fatigue; suicidal thoughts; appetite/ weight change; changed sleep pattern; retardation; agitation. The term 'masked depression' is used where patients with depressive disorder deny depressive mood. Degrees of severity of depression are identified.

Delirium. Characterised by disturbances of consciousness and attention, perception, thinking, memory, psychomotor behaviour, emotion and sleep patterns. More common after 60 years of age. The state is transient and fluctuating.

Dementia. Syndrome where disease of the brain, of chronic or progressive nature, leads to disturbances of multiple higher cortical functions, including memory and cognitive functions, commonly accompanied by disturbances of emotion and social behaviour.

Somatisation. A condition where the patient presents with a bodily symptom which is in fact without organic cause but a manifestation of an unacknowledged psychological problem, most commonly depression.

Chronic somatisation (chronic multiple unexplained symptoms). Patients who have chronic symptoms in numerous bodily systems which cannot be explained on the basis of organic illness. Typically manifests as repeated presentation of physical symptoms, repeated requests for medical investigations and reluctance to accept reassurance after negative findings. Also known as 'somatoform disorders'.

Factitious disorder. A less common condition where patients present with symptoms and signs that prove to be self-induced, but of no obvious benefit to the patient. Examples include self-induced skin lesions, self-induced abnormal laboratory results, laxative abuse, factitious pyrexia and Munchausen syndrome.

References

1   CREED F, MAYOU R, HOPKINS A, eds. *Medical symptoms not explained by organic disease.* London: Royal College of Psychiatrists and Royal College of Physicians of London, 1992.

2   MAYOU R, SMITH EBO. Hospital doctors' management of psychological problems. *British Journal of Psychiatry* 1986; **148**: 194–7.

3   MAYOU R, FEINMANN C, HODGSON G, JENKINS PL. The present state of consultation and liaison psychiatry. *Psychiatric Bulletin* 1990; **14**: 321–5.

4   HUYSE FJ. European Consultation-Liaison Workgroup. Consultation-liaison psychiatry: does it help to get organized? *General Hospital Psychiatry* 1991; **13**: 133–87.

5   KINGDON D. Mental health services: results of a survey of English district plans. *Psychiatric Bulletin* 1989; **13**: 77–8.

6   ROYAL COLLEGE OF PSYCHIATRISTS. *Mental health of the nation: the contribution of psychiatry.* Council Report CR16, 1992.

7   CREED F, GUTHRIE E, BLACK D, TRANMER M. Psychiatric referrals within the general hospital: comparison with referrals from general practitioners. *British Journal of Psychiatry* 1993; **162**: 204–11.

8   HOUSE A, CREED F. Training in liaison psychiatry. *Psychiatric Bulletin* 1993; **17**: 95–6.

9   WORLD HEALTH ORGANISATION. *Mental disorders: glossary and guide to their classification in accordance with the Ninth Revision of the International Classification of Diseases.* Geneva: WHO, 1978.

10   AMERICAN PSYCHIATRIC ASSOCIATION. *Diagnostic and statistical manual of mental disorders,* 3rd edn, revised. Washington: APA, 1987.

11   MAYOU RA, HAWTON KE. Psychiatric disorder in the general hospital. *British Journal of Psychiatry* 1986; **149**: 172–90.

12   FELDMAN E, MAYOU R, HAWTON K, ARDERN M, SMITH EBO. Psychiatric disorder in medical inpatients. *Quarterly Journal of Medicine* 1987; **63**: 405–12.

13   LADWIG KH, ROLL G, BREITHARDT G, BUDDE T, BORGGREFE M. Post-infarction depression and incomplete recovery 6 months after acute myocardial infarction. *Lancet* 1994; **343**: 20–3.

14   FRASURE-SMITH N, LESPÉRANCE F, TALAJIC M. Depression following myocardial infarction: impact on 6 month survival. *Journal of the American Medical Association* 1993; **270**: 1819–25.

15   HAWLEY DJ, WOLFE F. Anxiety and depression in patients with rheumatoid arthritis: a prospective study of 400 patients. *Journal of Rheumatology* 1988; **15**: 932–41.

16   CREED F. Psychological disorders in rheumatoid arthritis: a growing consensus. *Annals of Rheumatoid Disease* 1990; **49**: 808–12.

17   DROSSMAN DA, LESERMAN J, MITCHELL CM, LI ZM, *et al.* Health status and health care use in persons with inflammatory bowel disease. *Digestive Diseases and Sciences* 1991; **36**: 1746–55.

18   ROYAL COLLEGE OF PHYSICIANS Committee on Geriatrics. Report: Organic mental impairment in the elderly: implications for research, education and the provision of services. *Journal of the Royal College of Physicians of London* 1981; **15**: 141–67.

19   LIPOWSKI J. Delirium (acute confusional states). *Journal of the American Medical Association* 1987; **258**: 1789–92.

20   ROYAL COLLEGE OF PHYSICIANS OF LONDON and ROYAL COLLEGE OF PSYCHIATRISTS. *Care of elderly people with mental illness: specialist services and medical training.* Joint report, 1989.

21   HOLMES KM, SALTER RH, COLE TP, GIRDWOOD TG. A profile of district hospital gastroenterology. *Journal of the Royal College of Physicians of London* 1987; **21**: 111–4.

22   MAYOU RA. Atypical chest pain [review]. *Journal of Psychosomatic Research* 1989; **33**: 373–406.

23 HOPKINS A, MENKEN M, DeFRIESE G. A record of patient encounters in neurological practice in the United Kingdom. *Journal of Neurology, Neurosurgery and Psychiatry* 1989; **52**: 436–8.

24 KROENKE K, MANGELSDORFF AD. Common symptoms in ambulatory care: incidence, evaluation, therapy and outcome. *American Journal of Medicine* 1989; **86**: 262–6.

25 BARSKY AJ. Hidden reasons some patients visit doctors. *Annals of Internal Medicine* 1981; **94**: 492–8.

26 FITZPATRICK RM, HOPKINS A. Referrals to neurologists for headaches not due to structural disease. *Journal of Neurology, Neurosurgery and Psychiatry* 1981; **44**: 1061–7.

27 HEATON K. What makes people with abdominal pain consult their doctor? Chapter 1 (pp 1–8) in Reference 1, 1992.

28 KATON WJ, BUCHWALD DS, SIMON GE, RUSSO JE, MEASE PJ. Psychiatric illness in patients with chronic fatigue and those with rheumatoid arthritis. *Journal of General Internal Medicine* 1991; **6**: 277–85.

29 CREED F. Relationship of non-organic abdominal pain to psychiatric disorder and life stress. Chapter 2 (pp 9–16) in Reference 1, 1992.

30 BASS C, ed. *Somatisation: physical symptoms and psychological disorder.* Oxford: Blackwell Scientific Publications, 1990.

31 BRIDGES K, GOLDBERG D. Somatic presentation of DSM-III psychiatric disorders in primary care. *Journal of Psychosomatic Research* 1985; **29**: 563–9.

32 LLOYD G. *Textbook of general hospital psychiatry.* Edinburgh: Churchill Livingstone, 1991.

33 GOLDBERG D. The management of medical out-patients with non-organic disorders: the reattribution model. Chapter 7 (pp 53–59) in Reference 1, 1992.

34 LOPEZ-IBOR JJ. Masked depression. *British Journal of Psychiatry* 1972; **120**: 254–7.

35 STOUDEMIRE A, KAHN M, BROWN JT, LINFORS E, HOUPT JL. Masked depression in a combined medical-psychiatric unit. *Psychosomatics* 1985; **26**: 221–8.

36 PERKIN GD. An analysis of 7836 successive new outpatient referrals. *Journal of Neurology, Neurosurgery and Psychiatry* 1989; **52**: 447–8.

37 VAN HEMERT AM, HENGEVELD MW, BOLK JH, ROOIJMANS HG, VANDENBROUCKE JP. Psychiatric disorders in relation to medical illness among patients of a general medical outpatient clinic. *Psychological Medicine* 1993; **23**: 167–73.

38 CASSEM NH, BARSKY AJ. Functional somatic symptoms and somatoform disorders. In: Cassem NH, ed. *Massachusetts General Hospital handbook of general hospital psychiatry.* St Louis: Mosby Year Book, 1991.

39 FORD CV. *The somatising disorder: illness as a way of life.* New York: Elsevier Science, 1983.

40 ESCOBAR JI, GOLDING JM, HOUGH RL, KARNO M, *et al.* Somatization in the community: relationship to disability and use of services. *American Journal of Public Health* 1987; **77**: 837–40.

41 SIMON GE, VON KORFF M. Somatization and psychiatric disorder in the NIMH Epidemiologic Catchment Area study. *American Journal of Psychiatry* 1991; **148**: 1494–500.

42 HAMILTON J, CAMPOS R, CREED F. Anxiety, depression and management of medically unexplained symptoms in medical clinics. (Submitted for publication)

43 BASS C, MURPHY M. The chronic somatiser and the Government White Paper. *Journal of the Royal Society of Medicine* 1990; **83**: 203–5.

44 HEATLEY RV. Open access upper gastrointestinal endoscopy. *British Medical Journal* 1993; **306**: 1224.

45 FINK P. Mental illness and utilization of admission to general hospital: a register investigation. *Acta Psychiatrica Scandinavica* 1990; **82**: 458–62.

46 FINK P. The use of hospitalisations by persistent somatising patients. *Psychological Medicine* 1992; **22**: 173–80.

47 THOMAS C. Referrals to a British liaison psychiatry service. *Health Trends* 1983; **15**: 61–4.

48 KATON W, RIES RK, KLEINMAN A. Part II. A prospective DSM-III study of 100 consecutive somatization patients. *Comprehensive Psychiatry* 1984; **25**: 305–14.

49   SHAW J, CREED F. The cost of somatization. *Journal of Psychosomatic Research* 1991; **35**: 307–12.

50   QUINN MA, JOHNSTON RV. Alcohol problems in acute male medical admissions. *Health Bulletin* 1976; **34**: 253–6.

51   McINTYRE D. Alcohol-related problems among male patients admitted to a general medical ward: their identification and follow-up. *Health Bulletin* 1979; **37**: 213–7.

52   JARIWALLA AG, ADAMS PH, HORE BD. Alcohol and acute general medical admissions to hospital. *Health Trends* 1979; **11**: 95–7.

53   JARMAN CMB, KELLETT JM. Alcoholism in the general hospital. *British Medical Journal* 1979; **ii**: 469–72.

54   LLOYD G, CHICK J, CROMBIE E. Screening for problem drinkers among medical inpatients. *Drug and Alcohol Dependence* 1982; **10**: 355–9.

55   TAYLOR CL, KILBANE P, PASSMORE N, DAVIES R. Prospective study of alcohol-related admissions in an inner-city hospital. *Lancet* 1986; **ii**: 765–8.

56   LLOYD G, CHICK J, CROMBIE E, ANDERSON S. Problem drinkers in medical wards: consumption patterns and disabilities in newly identified male cases. *British Journal of Addiction* 1986; **81**: 789–95.

57   ROYAL COLLEGE OF PHYSICIANS. *A great and growing evil: the medical consequences of alcohol abuse.* London: Tavistock, 1987.

58   ROYAL COLLEGE OF PSYCHIATRISTS. *Alcohol: our favourite drug.* London: Tavistock, 1986.

59   ROYAL COLLEGE OF GENERAL PRACTITIONERS. *Alcohol: a balanced view.* London: RCGP, 1986.

60   FACULTY OF PUBLIC HEALTH MEDICINE. Royal College of Physicians. *Alcohol and the public health.* London: Macmillan Education Ltd, 1991.

61   GHODSE H. Drug related problems in London accident and emergency departments: a 12 month survey. *Lancet* 1981; **ii**: 859–62.

62   ROYAL COLLEGE OF PSYCHIATRISTS. *Drug scenes.* London: Gaskell, 1987.

63   BLACK D, CREED F. Assessment of self-poisoning patients by psychiatrists and junior medical staff. *Journal of the Royal Society of Medicine* 1988; **81**: 97–9.

64   OWENS D, DENNIS M, JONES S, DOVE A, DAVE S. Self-poisoning patients discharged from accident and emergency: risk factors and outcome. *Journal of the Royal College of Physicians of London* 1991; **25**: 218–22.

65   HOUSE A, OWENS D, STORER D. Psycho-social intervention following attempted suicide: is there a case for better services? *International Review of Psychiatry* 1992; **4**: 15–22.

66   SLAG MF, MORLEY JE, ELSON MK, TRENCE DL, *et al.* Impotence in medical clinic outpatients. *Journal of the American Medical Association* 1983; **249**: 1736–40.

67   MELMAN A, TIEFER L, PEDERSEN R. Evaluation of the first 406 patients in a urology department based centre for male sexual deviation. *Urology* 1988; **32**: 6–10.

68   KIRBY RS, CARSON C, WEBSTER GD. *Impotence: diagnosis and management of male erectile dysfunction.* Oxford: Butterworth Heinemann, 1991.

69   HAWTON K. Sexual problems in the general hospital. In: Creed FH, Pfeffer J, eds. *Medicine and psychiatry: a practical approach.* London: Pitman, 1982.

70   GUTHRIE E, CREED F, WHORWELL PJ. Severe sexual dysfunction in women with the irritable bowel syndrome: comparison with inflammatory bowel disease and duodenal ulceration. *British Medical Journal* 1987; **296**: 577–8.

71   WALKER EA, KATON W, HARROP-GRIFFITHS J, HOLM L, *et al.* Relationship of chronic pelvic pain to psychiatric diagnoses and childhood sexual abuse. *American Journal of Psychiatry* 1988; **145**: 75–80.

72   DROSSMAN DA, LESERMAN J, NACHMAN G, LI ZM, *et al.* Sexual and physical abuse in women with functional or organic gastrointestinal disorders. *Annals of Internal Medicine* 1990; **113**: 828–33.

73   BANCROFT J. *Human sexuality and its problems,* 2nd edn. Edinburgh: Churchill Livingstone, 1989.

74   BRIERE J. Methodological issues in the study of sexual abuse effects. *Journal of Consulting and Clinical Psychology* 1992; **60**: 196–203.

75 MAYOU R, SEAGROATT V, GOLDACRE M. Use of psychiatric services by patients in a general hospital. *British Medical Journal* 1991; **303**: 1029–32.

76 KATON W, VON KORFF M, LIN E, BUSH T, *et al.* A randomised trial of psychiatric consultation with distressed high utilizers. *General Hospital Psychiatry* 1992; **14**: 86–98.

77 GATER R, GOLDBERG D. Pathways to psychiatric care in South Manchester. *British Journal of Psychiatry* 1991; **159**: 90–6.

78 BRIDGES KW, GOLDBERG DP. Psychiatric illness in in-patients with neurological disorders: patients' views on discussion of emotional problems with neurologists. *British Medical Journal* 1984; **286**: 656–8.

79 DEROGATIS LR, ABELOFF MD, McBETH CD. Cancer patients and their physicians in the perception of psychological symptoms. *Psychosomatics* 1976; **17**: 197–201.

80 HARDMAN A, MAGUIRE P, CROWTHER D. The recognition of psychiatric morbidity on a medical oncology ward. *Journal of Psychological Research* 1989; **33**: 235–9.

81 SELTZER A. Prevalence, detection and referral of psychiatric morbidity in general medical patients. *Journal of the Royal Society of Medicine* 1989; **82**: 410–2.

82 BARRISON IG, VIOLA L, MURRAY-LYON IM. Do housemen take an adequate drinking history? *British Medical Journal* 1980; **281**: 1040.

83 ROWLAND N, MAYNARD A, BEVERIDGE A, KENNEDY P, *et al.* Doctors have no time for alcohol screening. *British Medical Journal* 1987; **295**: 95–6.

84 CHICK J, LLOYD G, CROMBIE E. Counselling problem drinkers in medical wards: a controlled study. *British Medical Journal* 1985; **290**: 965–7.

85 NUFFIELD INSTITUTE FOR HEALTH, University of Leeds. *Brief interventions and alcohol use.* Effective Health Care, Bulletin 7, 1993.

86 MAGUIRE GP, JULIER DL, HAWTON KE, GANCROFT J. Psychiatric morbidity and referral on two general medical wards. *British Medical Journal* 1974; **i**: 268–70.

87 MAGUIRE GP, LEE EG, BEVINGTON DJ, KÜCHEMANN CS, *et al.* Psychiatric problems in the first year after mastectomy. *British Medical Journal* 1978; **i**: 963–5.

88 DEVLEN J, MAGUIRE P, PHILLIPS P, CROWTHER D, CHAMBERS H. Psychological problems associated with diagnosis and treatment of lymphomas. I. Retrospective study. *British Medical Journal* 1987; **295**: 953–4.

89 MAGUIRE P. Barriers to the psychological care of the dying. *British Medical Journal* 1985; **291**: 1711–3.

90 ROSSER JE, MAGUIRE P. Dilemmas in general practice: the care of the cancer patient. *Social Science and Medicine* 1982; **16**: 315–22.

91 DELVAUX N, RAZAVI D, FARVACQUES C. Cancer care: a stress for health professionals. *Social Science and Medicine* 1988; **27**: 159–66.

92 WILKINSON S. Factors which influence how nurses communicate with cancer patients. *Journal of Advanced Nursing* 1991; **16**: 677–88.

93 MAGUIRE P, TAIT A, BROOKE M, THOMAS C, SELLWOOD R. Effect of counselling on the psychiatric morbidity associated with mastectomy. *British Medical Journal* 1980; **281**: 1454–6.

94 MAGUIRE P, FAULKNER A. How to improve the counselling skills of doctors and nurses in cancer care. *British Medical Journal* 1988; **297**: 847–9.

95 MAGUIRE P, BOOTH K, ELLIOTT C, HILLIER V. Helping cancer patients disclose their concerns. (Submitted for publication)

96 GOLDBERG D, GASK L, O'DOWD T. The treatment of somatization: teaching techniques of reattribution. *Journal of Psychosomatic Research* 1989; **32**: 137–44.

97 MEAKIN CJ. Screening for depression in the medically ill. *British Journal of Psychiatry* 1992; **160**: 212–6.

98 GOLDBERG D. Use of the general health questionnaire in clinical work. *British Medical Journal* 1986; **293**: 1188–9.

99 DEPARTMENT OF HEALTH AND SOCIAL SECURITY. *The management of deliberate self-harm.* Health Notice HN(84): 25. London: DHSS, 1984.

100 ROYAL COLLEGE OF PSYCHIATRISTS. *The general hospital management of adult deliberate self-harm: consensus statement on minimum standards for service provision*, 1994.

101 THOMPSON DR, MEDDIS R. A prospective evaluation of in-hospital counselling for first time myocardial infarction men. *Journal of Psychosomatic Research* 1990; **34**: 237–48.

102 FAVA GA. Depression in medical settings. In: Paykel ES, ed. *Handbook of affective disorders*, 2nd edn. Edinburgh: Churchill Livingstone, 1992: 667–85.

103 RODIN G, VOSHART K. Depression in the medically ill: an overview. *American Journal of Psychiatry* 1986; **143**: 696–705.

104 SERIES HG. Drug treatment of depression in medically ill patients. *Journal of Psychosomatic Research* 1992; **36**: 1–16.

105 LIPSEY JR, ROBINSON RG. PEARLSON GD, RAO K, PRICE TR. Nortriptyline treatment of post-stroke depression: a double-blind study. *Lancet* 1984; **i**: 297–300.

106 REDING MJ, ORTO LA, WINTER SW, FORTUNA IM, *et al.* Antidepressant therapy after stroke: a double-blind study. *Archives of Neurology* 1986; **43**: 763–5.

107 FEINMANN C. Antidepressants and their role in chronic pain: an update. Chapter 10 (pp 85–90) in Reference 1, 1992.

108 FRANCE RD. The future for antidepressants: treatment of pain. *Psychopathology* 1987; **20** (suppl 1): 99–113.

109 TARRIER N, MAGUIRE GP. Treatment of psychological distress following mastectomy: an initial report. *Behaviour Research and Therapy* 1983: **22**: 81–4.

110 GREER S. Cancer: psychiatric aspects. In: Granville-Grossman, ed. *Recent advances in clinical psychiatry*. Edinburgh: Churchill Livingstone, 1985.

111 GUTHRIE E, CREED F, DAWSON D, TOMENSON B. A controlled trial of psychological treatment for the irritable bowel syndrome. *Gastroenterology* 1990; **100**: 450–7.

112 KLIMES I, MAYOU RA. PEARCE MJ, COLES L, FAGG JR. Psychological treatment for atypical non-cardiac chest pain: a controlled evaluation. *Psychological Medicine* 1990; **20**: 605–11.

113 BUTLER S, CHALDER T, RON M, WESSLEY S. Cognitive behaviour therapy in chronic fatigue syndrome. *Journal of Neurology, Neurosurgery and Psychiatry* 1991; **54**: 153–8.

114 SALKOVSKIS P. The cognitive-behavioural approach. Chapter 9 (pp 70–84) in Reference 1, 1992

115 SHARPE M, PEVELER R, MAYOU R. The psychological treatment of patients with functional somatic symptoms: a practical guide. *Journal of Psychosomatic Research* 1992; **36**: 515–9.

116 SVEDLUND J, SJODIN I, OTTOSON JO, DOTEVALL G. Controlled study of psychotherapy in irritable bowel syndrome. *Lancet* 1983; **ii**: 589–92.

117 WHORWELL PJ, PRIOR A, FARAGHER EB. Controlled trial of hypnotherapy in the treatment of severe refractory irritable bowel syndrome. *Lancet* 1984; **ii**: 1232–4.

118 SMITH GR Jr, MONSON RA, RAY DC. Psychiatric consultation in somatization disorder: a randomized controlled study. *New England Journal of Medicine* 1986; **314**: 1407–13.

119 MARTIN RL, ROBERTS WV, CLAYTON PJ, WETZEL R. Psychiatric illness and non-cancer hysterectomy. *Diseases of the Nervous System* 1977; **38**: 974–80.

120 MURRAY GB. Chapter 6: Confusion, delirium and dementia. In: Cassem NH, ed. *Massachusetts General Hospital handbook of general hospital psychiatry*, 3rd edn, 1987: 89–120.

121 FULOP G, STRAIN JJ, VITA J, LYONS JS, HAMMER JS. Impact of psychiatric comorbidity on length of hospital stay for medical/surgical patients: a preliminary report. *American Journal of Psychiatry* 1987; **144**: 878–82.

122 HUYSE FJ, STRAIN JJ, HAMMER JS. Psychiatric comorbidity and length of hospital stay [letter]. *American Journal of Psychiatry* 1988; **145**: 1319.

123 THOMAS RI, CAMERON DJ, FAHS MC. A prospective study of delirium and prospective hospital stay. *Archives of General Psychiatry* 1988; **45**: 937–40.

124 ANDERSON R, FRANCIS A, LION J, DAUGHERTY V. Psychologically related illness and health services utilisation. *Medical Care* 1977; **15**: Suppl, 59–73.

125 LEVENSON JL, HAMER R, ROSSITER LF. Relation of psychopathology in general medical inpatients to use and cost of services. *American Journal of Psychiatry* 1990; **147**: 1498–503.

126 ACKERMAN AD, LYONS JS, HAMMER JS, LARSON DB. The impact of co-existing depression and timing of psychiatric consultation on medical patients' length of stay. *Hospital and Community Psychiatry* 1988; **39**: 173–6.

127 BARSKY AJ, WYSHAK G, KLERMAN GL. Medical and psychiatric determinants of out-patients medical utilisation. *Medical Care* 1986; **24**: 548–60.

128 LINN LS, YAGER J. Screening of depression in relationship to subsequent patient and physician behaviour. *Medical Care* 1982; **20**: 1233–40.

129 JONES KR, VISCHI TR. Impact of alcohol, drug abuse and mental health treatment on medical care utilisation: a review of the research literature. *Medical Care* 1979; **17** (suppl 2): 1–82.

130 STRAIN JJ, LYONS JS, HAMMER JS, FAHS M, *et al.* Cost offset from a psychiatric consultation-liaison intervention with elderly hip fracture patients. *American Journal of Psychiatry* 1991; **148**: 1044–9.

131 MUMFORD E, SCHLESINGER H, GLASS G, PATRICK C, CUERDON T. A new look at evidence about reduced cost of medical utilisation following mental health treatment. *American Journal of Psychiatry* 1984; **141**: 1145–58.

132 WALLACE P, CUTLER S, HAINES A. Randomized controlled trial of general practitioner intervention in patients with excessive alcohol consumption. *British Medical Journal* 1988; **297**: 663–8.

133 PETERS J, LARGE RG, ELKIND G. Follow-up results from a randomised controlled trial evaluating in- and out-patient pain management programmes. *Pain* 1992; **50**: 41–50.

134 SENSKY T, CUNDY T, GREER S, PETTINGALE KW. Referrals to psychiatrists in a general hospital: a comparison between two methods of liaison psychiatry. *Journal of the Royal Society of Medicine* 1985; **78**: 463–8.

135 TOREM M, SARAVAY S, STEINBERG H. Psychiatric liaison: benefits of an active approach. *Psychosomatics* 1979; **20**: 598–611.

136 STOLLER T, KNIGHT M. Chapter 13: The role of the social worker in liaison psychiatry. In: Creed F, Pfeffer JM, eds. *Medicine and psychiatry: a practical approach.* London: Pitman, 1982: 201–9.

137 FAUMAN MA. Psychiatric components of medical and surgical practice. II. Referral and treatment of psychiatric disorders. *American Journal of Psychiatry* 1983; **140**: 760–3.

138 SKUSE DH. Attitudes to the psychiatric outpatient clinic. *British Medical Journal* 1975; **iii**: 469–71.

139 RUMSEY N. Group stress management versus pharmacological treatment in the irritable bowel syndrome. In: Heaton K, Creed F, Goeting N, eds. *Towards confident management of irritable bowel syndrome.* Duphas Laboratories Ltd, 1991.

140 HARVEY RF, MAUAD EC, BROWN AM. Prognosis in the irritable bowel syndrome: a 5-year prospective study. *Lancet* 1987; **i**: 963–5.

141 MAGUIRE P, FAULKNER A. How to improve the counselling skills of doctors and nurses in cancer care. *British Medical Journal* 1988; **297**: 847–9.

142 WILKINSON S, MAGUIRE GP, TAIT A. Life after breast cancer. *Nursing Times* 1988; **84**: 34–7.

143 MARTEAU L. Chapter 3: The hospital: its staff and patients. In: Creed F, Pfeffer JM, eds. *Medicine and psychiatry: a practical approach.* London: Pitman, 1982: 38–50.

144 HALLETT EC, PILOWSKY I. The response to treatment in a multi-disciplinary pain clinic. *Pain* 1982; **12**: 365-74.

145 PETERS J, LARGE RG, ELKIND G. Follow-up results from a randomised control trial evaluating in- and out-patient pain management programmes. *Pain* 1992; **50**: 41–50.

146 BENJAMIN S, HOUSE A, JENKINS P. *Liaison psychiatry: defining needs and planning services.* London: Gaskell Press, 1994.

147 CREED FH, GUTHRIE E. Techniques for interviewing the somatising patient. *British Journal of Psychiatry* 1993; **162**: 467–71.

148 LLOYD GG, CAWLEY RH. Distress or illness? A study of psychological symptoms after myocardial infarction. *British Journal of Psychiatry* 1983; **142**: 120–5.

149 MOFFIC HS, PAYKEL ES. Depression in medical in-patients. *British Journal of Psychiatry* 1975; **126**: 346–53.

150 LLOYD GG, CAWLEY RH. Smoking habits after myocardial infarction. *Journal of the Royal College of Physicians of London* 1980; **14**: 224–6

151 PARKES CM. *Studies of grief in adult life.* Harmondsworth, England: Penguin Books, 1972: 36.

152 SHARPE M, BASS C. Pathophysiological mechanisms in somatization. *International Review of Psychiatry* 1992; **4**: 81–97.

153 GARDNER WN, BASS C. Hyperventilation in clinical practice. *British Journal of Hospital Medicine* 1989; **41**: 73–81.

154 GOLDBERG DP, BRIDGES K. Somatic presentations of psychiatric illness in primary care settings. *Journal of Psychosomatic Research* 1988; **32**: 137–44.

155 GOLDBERG DP, BENJAMIN S, CREED F. *Psychiatry in medical practice,* 2nd edn. London, New York: Routledge, 1994.

156 PERKIN GD. An analysis of 7836 successive new outpatient referrals. *Journal of Neurology, Neurosurgery and Psychiatry* 1989; **52**: 447–8.

157 BLACKWELL B. Illness behaviour labelling and compliance. *Clinical and Investigative Medicine* 1981; **4**: 209–14.

158 MECHANIC D. The concept of illness behaviour. *Journal of Chronic Disorders* 1961; **15**: 184–94.

159 GOLDBERG DP. *The detection of psychiatric illness by questionnaire.* Oxford: Oxford University Press, 1972.

160 ZIGMOND A, SNAITH R. The hospital anxiety and depression scale. *Acta Psychiatrica Scandinavica* 1983; **67**: 361–70.

161 NOYES R, REICH J, CLANCY J, O'GORMAN T. Reduction of hypochondriasis with treatment of panic disorder. *British Journal of Psychiatry* 1986; **149**: 631–5.

162 PILOWSKI I, MURRELL TGC, GORDON A. The development of a screening method for abnormal illness behaviour. *Journal of Psychosomatic Research* 1979; **23**: 203–7.

163 BECK AT, SCHUYLER D, HERMAN J. Development of suicide intent scales. In: Beck AT, Ressik HLP, Lettieri DJ, eds. *The prediction of suicide.* Maryland: Charles Press, 1974.

164 FOLSTEIN MF, FOLSTEIN SE, McHUGH PR. Mini-mental state: a practical method for grading the cognitive state of patients for the clinician. *Journal of Psychiatric Research* 1975; **12**: 189–98.

165 BLESSED G, ROTH M, TOMLINSON B. The association between quantitative measures of dementia and senile changes in the grey matter. *British Journal of Psychiatry* 1986; **114**: 797–811.

166 MAYOU R. Patients' fears of illness: chest pain and palpitations. Chapter 4 (pp 25–33) in Reference 1, 1992.

167 CREED FH, MAYOU R, FRIEDMAN T, *et al.* The European Consultation-Liaison Study: UK result. (In preparation)

168 BECK AT, WARD CH, MENDELSON M, MOCK J, ERBAUGH J. An inventory for measuring depression. *Archives of General Psychiatry* 1961; **4**: 561–71.

169 BERNARDT M, TAYLOR C, MUMFORD J, SMITH B, BURRAY R. Comparison of questionnaire and laboratory tests in the detection of excessive drinking and alcoholism. *Lancet* 1982; **i**: 325–8.

170 BENDALL MJ. Current medical literature. *Geriatrics* 1988; **1**: 2–7.

171 BUGLASS D, HORTON J. A scale for predicting subsequent suicidal behaviour. *British Journal of Psychiatry* 1974; **124**: 573–8.

172 GLASSMAN AH, BIGGER JT, GIARDINA EV, KANTOR SJ, *et al.* Clinical characteristics of imipramine-induced orthostatic hypotension. *Lancet* 1979; **i**: 468–72.

173 WATTIS JP. Geographical variations in the provision of psychiatric services for old people. *Age and Ageing* 1988; **17**: 171–80.